CORE
and the Strategy of Nonviolence

RANDOM HOUSE STUDIES IN SOCIOLOGY

Consulting Editor
PETER I. ROSE, *Smith College*

CORE

and the Strategy of Nonviolence

INGE POWELL BELL

Pitzer College, The Claremont Colleges

RANDOM HOUSE

New York

Foreword

BY JAMES FARMER

It is difficult to imagine a more timely study than Inge Bell's on the strategy of nonviolence. With destruction erupting in urban streets and violence heralded as being "as American as cherry pie," the pacifistic voices of Gandhi and Martin Luther King seem terribly remote.

For CORE, nonviolence—never a way of life, but only a strategy —ended on a balmy night, September 1, 1963, in a sleepy town on the Mississippi, when a uniformed mob screamed for my blood. The casketless hearse in which I escaped became for CORE a symbol of the burial of peace.

"We are with you," said a couple of my staff workers, black and young, "but if there comes another night like that, we will have our hardware ready."

The massive violence of bigotry became the killer of the dream of passive resistance. Replacing that dream was the doctrine of self-defense—a concept that in itself is harmless and thoroughly "American," for the ethos of this nation is not nonresistance. But the trouble with "defense" is that a dim line divides it from retaliatory and offensive violence. Whites and blacks "defend" themselves against each other and the cycle seems endless.

That is the crux of the problem of race in America today: not that black people are violent, but that the whole nation is wedded to the notion that "the big fist wins."

We are indebted to Dr. Bell for bringing to bear the discipline and skills of the social scientist in examining the Americanization of the movement. She has illuminated the past and helped clarify the present.

Acknowledgments

I am very deeply indebted to Professor William Kornhauser for the meticulous reading and agonizing, though always useful, criticism he gave the manuscript during its initial preparation as a dissertation. My thanks also go to the other members of my dissertation committee, Professors Reinhard Bendix and Charles Sellers, for their guidance.

Dorothy Mariner, Dorothy Smith, Robert Alford, Hanan C. Selvin, and Genevieve Hughes all helped me at various points by offering criticism of the manuscript and advice and help in its preparation for publication.

Dr. Peter Rose, who was the academic editor, deserves my sincere thanks for prodding and plaguing me into many important and valuable revisions.

The National Institute of Mental Health provided a grant that enabled me to write the manuscript, and the University of California at Berkeley provided summer travel grants that made the Southern field work possible.

I reserve my deepest gratitude for the many CORE leaders and members who offered me the hospitality of their homes, the warmth of their friendship, and many long hours of their time. As a researcher, I was singularly fortunate to work among people of such exceptionally generous spirit. I hope they can forgive me my critical insights. Above all, I hope they can forgive me for reducing their beautiful human realities to sociological categories and hypotheses. My life has been permanently enriched by this encounter with the young activists of the civil rights movement. May their dream yet come true.

Contents

CORE

and the Strategy of Nonviolence

CHAPTER 1

Prologue

Protest against the oppression of the American Negro is as old as slavery. Violent organized slave uprisings occurred from time to time throughout the two and a half centuries of slavery. More common, though less dramatic, were instances of violence, poisoning, and arson by which individual slaves reacted against white oppression. Newspapers of the pre-Civil War period attest to the frequency with which slaves ran away from their masters—a trickle that turned into a stream with the emergence of the underground railroad, an illegal network through which Northern white abolitionists and runaway slaves helped 75,000 slaves escape to freedom in the northern United States and Canada. Led by whites like William Lloyd Garrison and Negroes like Frederick Douglass, the abolitionist movement gained considerable Northern support for its attacks on the institution of slavery during the decades preceding the Civil War and helped to bring about the emancipation of slaves during the war.[1]

For twelve years after the war's end, the federal government, backed by strong anti-Southern sentiment in the North, prevented the old Southern slave-owning aristocracy from regaining political control. Negroes were guaranteed the franchise and protected in their exercise of citizenship rights and their use of public and private accommodations. This era came to an end with the withdrawal of Northern occupation troops in the political compromise of 1876. Northern industrialists and political leaders had decided to make peace with Southern landholders and once again abandoned the Negro to their control.[2]

During the 1880s and 1890s, the complicated structure of Jim Crow law and custom was established to return the Negro, as nearly as possible, to the slave status from which he had so lately emerged. Laws were passed to segregate Negroes in every type of community institution—from schools, parks, and hospitals to funeral homes and cemeteries. In the majority of instances "segregation" simply meant relegating Negroes to the use of inferior accommodations or barring them altogether from any facilities. Simultaneously a series of legal and informal devices effectively barred all Negroes from the vote, jury duty, militia service, and every other privilege of citizenship. Almost all occupations above those of sharecropper and unskilled worker were closed to the Negro, and most of the landless Negro farmers were reduced to a state of permanent indebtedness.[3]

The campaign to resubordinate the Negro was marked by the extensive use of terror and violence. During some periods of the 1890s, a Negro lynching was reported every two days in the South.[4] These were the dark days when Booker T. Washington attained white-sponsored prominence as the accommodationist leader who strove to reconcile the Negro to his disenfranchised and oppressed lot in return for meager white support for the training of young Negroes in domestic and agricultural skills.

The Southern Negro was effectively silenced. But in the North, the militant Negro scholar W. E. B. Du Bois bitterly attacked Washington's accommodationism and laid the groundwork for the long struggle toward full manhood and equal citizenship. In 1909 he joined with a group of predominantly white sympathizers to found the National Association for the Advancement of Colored People. The NAACP's first nationwide campaign was for the passage of federal anti-lynch legislation. Southern filibusters blocked passage of such legislation in the Senate, but the long campaign to publicize the frequency and savagery of Southern lynching helped to decrease this atrocious practice.[5]

The Universal Negro Improvement Association, a black nationalist movement led by Jamaica-born Marcus Garvey, emerged during the period between the two world wars. Although Garvey's program of creating separate Negro businesses and eventual return of the American Negroes to Africa failed to be implemented, the movement drew the largest mass following attained by any Negro movement before or since. Appealing mainly to lower class Negroes in Northern cities, the UNIA printed a newspaper with a circulation of 200,000 and claimed membership of over 2 million persons of African descent in America and throughout the world.[6]

During the Depression, direct action and boycott campaigns developed sporadically in Northern cities. Chicago's "spend your money where you can work" campaign was typical of these attempts to obtain some economic advantages for the Negro.[7] The first nationwide use of nonviolent direct action, however, came with the end of the Depression in 1941. Though always on the bottom of the ladder, the Negro had at least shared the burden of unemployment with many whites during the 1930s, but with the economic upswing brought on by war preparation, he now saw the signs on the factory gates change from "No Help Wanted" to "Men Wanted—Whites Only." At the same time, Negro men from Northern cities were being drafted to fight Hitlerism and sent for military training to the Deep South, where they were frequently met with hostility and violence. In response to this situation, A. Philip Randolph, the leading Negro labor union leader, organized a nationwide march on Washington movement. He threatened to march 100,000 Negroes to Washington to tie up the capital unless the President signed an executive order guaranteeing fair employment practices in war industries. Randolph's threat succeeded in forcing the creation of the Federal Fair Employment Practices Commission, and the march was called off.[8]

Direct Action Emerges

Between the founding of the NAACP in 1909 and its great court victory in 1954, civil rights activity had switched its focus several times in an effort to escape the barriers inherent in white-controlled political institutions. The initial emphasis on Congress was abandoned after the failure to obtain a federal antilynch law, and pressure shifted to the executive, where it succeeded in winning the executive order establishing the Fair Employment Practices Commission. But Congress weakened the FEPC almost immediately and forced its dismantling in 1946. Now the focus of hope and pressure shifted to the courts, which were less hampered by majority opinion.

In 1933 the NAACP began a series of lawsuits to equalize expenditures for the separate and supposedly equal Southern school system. At the beginning of this campaign, the average per capita annual expenditure for Negro children in Southern schools was $12, compared with $45 for white children. The cases were fought in state after state and city after city and succeeded in bringing about partial equalization of the two school systems. In the late 1930s, the NAACP switched its strategy to an attack on school segregation as such, a drive that culminated in the 1954 Supreme Court decision in the case of *Brown vs. Board of Education,* in which the Court ruled that segregated schools are inherently unequal because they imply the inferiority of the Negro child. Although the 1954 decision was limited to educational facilities, it applied, by implication, to all tax-supported facilities. Indeed, most Negroes took it as a statement from the highest authority in the land that segregation was inherently unconstitutional.[9]

The final victory of this legal campaign was won in 1954. But with the victory came the beginning of the disillusionment with this, the last established avenue of appeal. It quickly became clear that the 1954 decision would be neither obeyed by Southern states nor vigorously enforced by the federal government. Implementation of the decision proceeded at such a slow rate that by 1963 only 0.8 percent of Southern Negro children were attending integrated schools.[10] In the North, meanwhile, housing discrimination, poverty, and postwar unemployment drew ever tighter lines around the growing ghettos and created de facto segregated schools at an increasing rate.[11] Every established political avenue had been proved incapable of bringing about any significant change in the Negro's condition. The greatest progress had come as a result of World War II, and, aside from a slight assist from the Fair Employment Practices Act, it had come entirely through the impersonal and unintended forces of the labor market, which, in its dire need for wartime manpower, had opened up many industrial jobs for the first time to Negroes and drawn hundreds of thousands of Negroes out of low-paying Southern agriculture into better-paying Northern and Southern industry.

During the mid-fifties Negro protest reached an incipient crisis. Since the beginning of World War II the Negro community had been undergoing a "revolution of rising expectations." The 1954 school desegregation decision itself contributed to this mood. Most Negroes regarded the decision as a great victory and expected its rapid implementation. The impression made by the decision and the way in which its nonimplementation contributed to the Negro mood is expressed in the recollections of one young CORE member:

> I was in the eighth grade and when I went to school the day after the decision, our teacher told us to get prepared. She told us we should study more—and we were all expecting it to happen next year. But of course we graduated before anything went into effect. After a while I didn't think we'd get it any

more. I used to think about it a lot because I had to go past a white school to get to my school and we were just going half-day then. I wanted to get into the other school.

Louis Lomax describes how unable Negroes were to believe that the decision would not be enforced:

> Let me state it in terms of typical Negro naïveté: It was incredible to a Negro woman who had been a servant in a white home for twenty years that her employers would cringe and hide while white trash threw bricks at her grandson on his way to school.[12]

The long NAACP legal campaign to equalize school expenditures had succeeded in producing a generation of Southern Negro youngsters confident of their capacity to enter white schools and white jobs, yet barred at every turn by the Jim Crow system. The northward migration of Negroes during World War II and the decline of terrorism against Negroes in the South had produced, in both the North and the South, a generation uncowed by the intimidation that had driven most of their elders into a quiet struggle for mere survival.

Finally, and perhaps most fundamentally, the end of colonialism in most African areas and the emergence of African nations and their leaders into independence and world prominence profoundly affected the self-image of the new Negro generation. The global hegemony of the white man had been broken after 400 years. The moral and aesthetic superiority of white civilization was being actively questioned and denied by new nations that had thrown off the colonial yoke. The young Negro identified his struggle with that of the African nations, and their victories kindled his hopes.

Against these rising expectations was frustration born of the realization that none of the established political channels would enable the Negro to make any significant progress. One by one they had failed to deliver. The small increases of status won through equalization of school expenditures and northward migration did not even begin to fill the growing gap between expectations and reality. A new outlet for the push toward equality had to be found. It was direct action.

The first significant break came in Montgomery, Alabama, on December 5, 1955, when local Negroes, outraged at the continual humiliation and mistreatment suffered at the hands of armed bus drivers on the city's segregated bus system, began their year-long boycott. The desegregation decision came finally through the courts rather than through boycott pressure. But the great significance of the Montgomery boycott was that for the first time direct action was raised to the level of a new strategy, superior to the old political and legal methods. By linking direct action with the philosophy of nonviolence, Martin Luther King provided the civil rights movement with a stirring new philosophy and set the ideological cornerstone for the direct action movement.[13]

In 1957 King founded the Southern Christian Leadership Conference, an association whose leadership largely was made up of Negro and white clergymen, which was to become one of the three nationwide organizations leading the nonviolent direct action movement.[14]

Direct action exploded into a Southern-wide movement in February, 1960, when a small group of Negro college students sat down at a segregated dime store lunch counter in Greensboro, North Carolina, and refused to move until they were served. After their first experience, the students called in organizers from the New York office of the Congress of Racial Equality to train them in methods of nonviolent direct action. Like a brush fire sweeping across parched hillsides, the sit-in movement spread to every state of the upper and lower South. In the North, supporting groups were formed and sympathetic picket lines appeared in front of the affected nationwide chain stores in every major city. During the following year, the movement involved as many as 70,000 demonstrators, who staged over 800 sit-ins in over a hundred cities. Between 3,600 and 4,000 demonstrators were arrested. As a direct result, restaurants in eight major cities were desegregated.[15] In May, 1960, the Southern Negro students who had sparked the sit-in movement formed the Student Nonviolent Coordinating Committee to coordinate the activity of their local groups. The second of the nationwide direct action organizations had emerged. Within three years SNCC was to grow into an organization with 150 full-time employees and a budget of a quarter of a million dollars.[16]

CORE's Role in the Direct Action Movement

Nonviolent direct action had come into its own. The Congress of Racial Equality, third of the big direct action organizations, remained relatively unknown until the following year, when it was named in national headlines as the major sponsor of the freedom rides. Yet by 1960, CORE was already eighteen years old—the oldest and most experienced of the direct action groups. It was founded in Chicago in 1942 by James Farmer, then Race Relations Secretary for the Fellowship of Reconciliation, a pacifist group founded by Quakers and Episcopalians during World War I. Farmer, a young Negro minister and labor organizer; James R. Robinson, a white pacifist; and a small group of FOR members and University of Chicago students decided to try applying Gandhi's technique of nonviolent resistance to American race relations. By sitting-in and picketing they succeeded in desegregating several Chicago restaurants.

Supported by help from the Fellowship of Reconciliation, CORE began forming chapters in St. Louis, Baltimore, New York, Los Angeles, and a few other Northern and Border State cities. The first direct action projects were carefully and patiently planned. In St. Louis and Baltimore, several years of direct action effort desegregated downtown lunch counters and restaurants. Farmer describes CORE in these early years as

> small, Northern, middle-class, elitist, idealistic, and predominantly white. We had not yet heard the voice of the masses. Nor, for that matter, had many people heard us. Until 1956 we survived entirely as a volunteer organization to which we were all able to give only part of our time. We had no budget to speak of and no organized publicity.[17]

Some of the early campaigns were marked by arrests and violence. In 1947 CORE and FOR cosponsored a "journey of reconciliation" into the upper South. An integrated team of sixteen persons set out on a two-week trip on Greyhound and Trailways buses to test implementation of the 1946 Supreme Court decision that outlawed segregation aboard buses engaged in interstate travel. The ride ended in arrest, with three men serving thirty-day sentences on Southern road gangs.[18] A CORE campaign to desegregate Palisades Amusement Park in New Jersey in 1947–1948 led to repeated arrests and violence against the nonviolent demonstrators.[19]

In the late 1950s CORE activity moved southward. Jim McCain, a Negro school principal and CORE member, began a voter registration campaign in his home state, South Carolina. In 1959 sit-ins were carried out as far south as Marion, South Carolina, and Miami, Florida.[20]

During 1960, when the sit-in movement swept through Southern Negro colleges, the patient, measured pace of CORE quickened as the organization hurried to keep up with the exploding activities of a new Negro generation. With the freedom rides of the summer of 1961, CORE shot into national prominence as a major force in the new civil rights movement.

The idea for the freedom rides grew out of a 1960 Supreme Court decision that extended the interstate travel ruling to cover terminal facilities used by passengers in interstate travel. On May 4 thirteen CORE members set out to test waiting rooms, rest rooms, and restaurants in bus terminals from Washington, D.C., to New Orleans. From the time they reached North Carolina, the riders were subjected to arrests and intermittent violence. And, on the morning of May 15, Americans across the country opened their newspapers and saw a front-page picture of a burning bus—a huge cloud of black smoke rising above the wreckage, on which the caption "travel in comfort and leave the driving to us" could still be clearly read. The bus had been set afire by a white mob outside of Anniston, Alabama, on May 14, Mother's Day. The freedom riders and other passengers scrambled out the windows to safety. A second group of riders upon their arrival in Birmingham was beaten by a mob. There, the battered little group reassembled and flew to New Orleans. The first lap of the freedom ride had ended.[21]

Almost immediately a student group in Nashville set out to complete the interrupted ride. After encountering violence in Montgomery, they were joined by CORE leaders from New York, and they all pressed on to Jackson, where they were immediately arrested.* Now the cry went up to fill the jails of Mississippi with freedom riders in the hope that the attendant publicity would compel the federal government to enforce compliance with the Supreme Court desegregation rulings. CORE, SNCC, the Southern Christian Leadership Conference, and the Nashville Student Movement had recruited and trained more than 300 freedom riders now bound for the state penitentiary at Parchman, Mississippi.

The freedom rides led to an Interstate Commerce Commission ruling on September 22, 1961, implementing the Supreme Court decision with new penalties for noncompliance. Although CORE teams testing out the new rulings were still

* The NAACP Legal Defense and Education Fund contributed heavily to the bail and legal defense of the riders.

destined to suffer imprisonment and violence in small Southern towns, the major battle for desegregation of interstate commerce had been won. As a result of the dramatic events of 1961, CORE's budget jumped from $233,000 to $750,000.[22] The increase in chapters and membership consisted of a disproportionate increase in Southern chapters and Negro members. By 1962 the organization had changed from predominantly white membership to one almost equally balanced between whites and Negroes.[23]

During the spring and summer of 1962, CORE launched a massive campaign to correct another injustice in interstate travel: Jim Crow restaurants along the major highways of the South. South of Washington, D.C., Negro motorists often had to go along the highway for many weary hours, sometimes whole days, before finding a restaurant that would serve them. The "freedom highways" drive organized demonstrations at dozens of establishments along highways in Florida, Virginia, and North Carolina. More than eighty restaurants, including the Howard Johnson and Holiday Inn chains in these areas, were opened to Negro customers as a result of the drive.[24] Although hundreds of demonstrators participated and scores were arrested, the campaign received much less publicity than the freedom rides of the previous summer.

The first of the "long hot summers" came in 1963. Peaceful mass demonstrations led by Martin Luther King in Birmingham exploded into violence when Negro youths who were not involved in the organized demonstrations began to fight back against police violence. More than a million persons throughout the country attended solidarity demonstrations for the Negro movement in Birmingham.

In August more than 200,000 civil rights backers staged the "march on Washington" to demonstrate the Negro's newfound organizational power and to dramatize the demand for a federal civil rights act. While the violence in Birmingham and the march on Washington took center stage, civil rights action everywhere hit an all-time high. During the three-month summer period, the Justice Department counted 1,412 separate demonstrations and 12,500 arrests in connection with civil rights activities. Some 6,000 people participated in a single CORE demonstration in Greensboro, North Carolina, alone. As a result of the summer's activity, 275 of the 574 Southern communities with populations of 10,000 or more desegregated some of their facilities.[25]

While CORE groups around the country were pursuing local campaigns, the national CORE office launched another summer project: voter registration and desegregation in several southern Louisiana parishes, including Iberville Parish, where the town of Plaquemine is located. James Farmer, CORE's national director, sent his greetings to the march on Washington from a jail in Plaquemines Parish. Soon after his release, he led another march in Plaquemine, which was attacked by mounted state troopers using cattle prods and tear gas. The demonstrators and Farmer took refuge in a Negro funeral home while the troopers forced their way into house after house in the Negro community looking for Farmer, whom they had loudly vowed to kill. Farmer escaped to New Orleans in a hearse driven by two local Negroes.[26]

In 1963 a new organization, the Council of Federated Organizations (COFO), was set up to coordinate a Mississippi voter registration drive by SNCC, CORE, SCLC, the NAACP, and various local civil rights groups. The project was backed by a large grant given by the Taconic Foundation and administered by the Southern Regional Council.[27] During the 1963 gubernatorial election in Mississippi, the Student Nonviolent Coordinating Committee organized a "freedom vote" campaign, in which 93,000 Negroes "voted" in a mock election designed to demonstrate to the country that Negroes were not indifferent to their exclusion from the franchise. Many white college students traveled to Mississippi for a few weeks to help in the campaign. After the "election," it was decided that during the coming summer Mississippi would need a massive influx of Northern civil rights workers to push voter registration. COFO took charge of the drive, which recruited 800 Northern students for the Mississippi "freedom summer" drive. Most of the volunteers were white, partly because they were able to pay their own travel expenses and provide their own money for a bail fund. The freedom summer project was marked by literally hundreds of arrests and beatings and the deaths of three young CORE workers, one Negro and two whites, who were brutally slain in Neshoba County, Mississippi.

During that same summer a new political party was organized: the Mississippi Freedom Democratic party, with branches in forty counties. The aim of the MFDP was to launch a campaign to unseat the regular all-white segregationist Mississippi delegation at the Democratic national convention in favor of the delegates from the Freedom Democratic party. Numerous Northern delegations came to the convention pledged to back this demand, but with Barry Goldwater nominated on the Republican ticket the Southern delegates were able to threaten a bolt from the party. Consequently, the MFDP candidates were offered a weak compromise: two "at-large" delegate positions. They refused the offer and demonstrated by sitting down in the regular Mississippi delegates' section while SNCC and CORE demonstrated outside.

During the years 1961–1964, CORE chapters in the North escalated their campaigns against discrimination in employment, housing, and schools. National and regional boycotts were launched to end employment discrimination in large firms. The nationwide campaign against Sears Roebuck in 1962 and the West Coast campaigns against Lucky Stores and Bank of America were among many such efforts that attained at least partial success in opening jobs to Negroes. In New York during the summer of 1963, CORE tried to halt work on $2.5 billion worth of city and state building construction in order to force the hiring of Negroes and Puerto Ricans in the highly discriminatory building trades jobs. Hundreds of New York CORE members were arrested as they lay down in front of bulldozers, and others staged a forty-four day sit-in at City Hall.[28] In a similar construction site demonstration in Cleveland, the Reverend Bruce Klunder, a white CORE member, was killed when a bulldozer accidentally backed over his body.[29]

Housing demonstrations were organized to protest dilapidated housing and inadequate city services in the Negro ghetto. Discriminatory realtors and subdivision builders were attacked with picket lines, sit-ins, and "dwell-ins." In Sacramento, California, for several weeks during the summer of 1963, CORE demonstrators sat-in around the clock at the State Capital rotunda to force passage of a fair housing act. CORE joined with other organizations in backing mass school boycotts protesting de facto segregation and inadequate conditions in Northern ghetto schools.

When the New York World's Fair opened on April 22, 1964, some 750 CORE demonstrators protesting discrimination in New York City swarmed over the fairgrounds, blocking entrances, climbing on exhibits, and drowning out President Johnson's opening speech with chants of "Freedom

Now." Some 300 demonstrators, including such nationally prominent figures as James Farmer, Bayard Rustin, and Michael Harrington, were arrested. Fair officials were horrified and television viewers were doubtless impressed and sometimes outraged at the spectacle. Yet most of New York breathed a sigh of relief, for the massive demonstrations represented a victory for the forces of moderation in CORE. Several of the militant New York chapters had advocated the much more drastic tactic of bringing New York City to a halt on that opening day by stalling automobiles on the major highways and pulling emergency switches on subways. These threats cut the expected attendance on the fair's opening day in half, but the stall-ins failed to materialize, partly because of the opposition of the national CORE leadership.[30]

By the summer of 1964, CORE had grown into a large, nationwide organization with a budget of almost $900,000.[31] The racial composition of the organization had also changed. Although most of the financial contributors were white,[32] the active chapter members now were predominantly Negro, and Negroes everywhere were asserting their right to leadership. By 1964 it had become almost impossible for a white person to be elected chairman of a chapter, though one might serve as chairman of a committee.[33]

The drive to desegregate public accommodations in the South culminated in the passage of the Civil Rights Act in July, 1964. The most important section of this historic act outlawed discrimination in most types of hotels, restaurants, and theaters. Other sections empowered the federal government to halt funds to federally aided programs that discriminated; forbade voter registrars from applying different standards to Negroes and whites; outlawed discrimination by employers and unions in certain types of employment; and empowered the attorney general to initiate suits in behalf of aggrieved persons in various discriminatory situations.[34] Although some civil rights leaders correctly argued that many sections of the new act were already covered under older constitutional and legal provisions that only required enforcement by federal authorities, there is no doubt that the public accommodations provision produced a real change throughout most of the South.

But the summer of 1964 also brought the first serious signs of white reaction: the Republican party nominated Barry Goldwater, conservative defender of "state's rights," as its presidential candidate, and the response of many liberals and leading Democrats was to call for a moratorium on direct action for the duration of the campaign. Although CORE and the Student Nonviolent Coordinating Committee refused to agree to the moratorium, the election campaign drained the efforts of pro-civil rights forces in both the white and the Negro communities. The Southern Regional Council reported that demonstrations during the preelection period fell to one-fourth of the number held during the same period of the previous year.[35]

The passage of the Civil Rights Act and the Goldwater campaign both had the effect of cutting CORE's income. Many white supporters felt that, with the passage of the act, the major battle had been won and support was no longer necessary. Many others, threatened by the possibility of a Goldwater victory, threw all their financial resources behind the Johnson campaign. During 1964 the national CORE office developed a $200,000 deficit, which by 1966 had grown to over $300,000. The staff had to be cut, and various regional offices closed down.

CORE's Changing Role in the Negro Community

In 1964 CORE began to turn increasingly from direct action to community organization in the black ghettos of America's big cities. The race riots that swept through many Northern ghettos during the summers of 1964, 1965, and 1966 dramatized to CORE leaders their lack of contact with the lower class Negro masses; the predominantly middle class, integrated CORE groups had never been able to appeal to them. Most of CORE's activities, particularly in the North, had been directed toward opening middle class jobs and middle income housing. In addition, CORE's nonviolent, integrationist philosophy was not congenial to the Northern ghetto, and the direct action technique required a kind of political sophistication that was quite alien to the experiences of many lower class persons.

In order to bridge the chasm between themselves and the mass of ghetto dwellers, Negro CORE leaders turned increasingly to the building up of community centers, skills training centers, and other types of community organizations with immediate appeal to ghetto residents. This approach was strongly encouraged by the federal government's "war on poverty," which made money available for the development of such programs.

The new direction of CORE strategy automatically weakened the role of whites in the organization, for it was difficult for them to function in the race-conscious ghetto. In order to appeal to the mood of lower class Negroes, CORE workers began to de-emphasize integration as a goal. Sensing the great psychological needs of lower class Negroes for group cohesion and race pride, CORE began to adopt many of the slogans and arguments that the black nationalists had used so successfully in their appeal to the Negro masses. The ideology of nonviolence, too, made little sense to the ghetto inhabitants, whose way of life was riddled with violence and who saw in nonviolence merely another version of the humility and passivity demanded of the Negro throughout his long subordination in America. This element of CORE philosophy was also increasingly played down or eliminated.

Simultaneous with these changes within CORE, the influence of the "new left," with its disdain for the liberal "establishment" and its radical criticism of the "corporate liberalism" dominating American society, functioned to drive still deeper the wedge between the white liberal allies of integration and the CORE workers in the ghettos. One of the important developments growing out of the convergence of new left criticism and growing Negro nationalism was the emergence in the South of Negro political parties that were independent of Democratic party alliances and that openly asserted the Negro's right of self-defense against Southern lawlessness.

These radicalizing developments brought about a dramatic change of policy in CORE at its 1966 national convention. The slogan "black power" was taken up as the theme of the convention. "Black power" meant two things: emphasis on the cohesion and race pride of the Negro community; and the building up of political power through independent Negro voting blocs that would not be bound to the Democratic party but would drive a hard bargain with both parties and serve as a third force when necessary. The slogan was part of a concerted effort to appeal to the ghetto even if it meant losing white financial backing. As part of the same attempt, the 1966 convention renounced absolute nonviolence and announced that, henceforth, the doctrine of nonviolence would not be interpreted as abrogating the "natural and constitutional right of self-defense."

In looking at the history of CORE, we may distinguish three distinct periods, marked by different tactics, different goals, and a different composition of membership.

The first period, from 1942 until the freedom rides in 1961, might be termed the era of *small-scale direct action*. The emphasis during this period was on strict nonviolence; the organization was predominantly white, Northern, and upper middle class. The major goal was integration of public accommodations.

The second period, from 1961 until 1964, might be called the era of *mass direct action*. Though nonviolence continued to be accepted as a tactic, emphasis shifted from nonviolent goodwill to the organization of coercive pressure through massive direct action demonstrations. During this period, the organization became more evenly balanced between Negro and white and Northern and Southern members. The emphasis began to shift from public accommodations to such new concerns as fair employment, open housing, and voter registration.

The third period, which first began to crystallize in 1964, might well be termed the era of *ghetto organization*. The fight to open middle class jobs and housing, and the concern with integration of public facilities—always more of a middle class than a working class issue in the Negro community—has given way to a drive to alleviate the plight of the lower class. Black power—economic and political—has replaced integration as the goal of CORE's activities. Nonviolence has given way to the assertion of the right of self-defense. Direct action has been largely replaced by community and political organization in the ghetto. The membership of CORE has become predominantly Negro and increasingly working class.

NOTES

1. On the history of slavery see Kenneth Stampp, *The Peculiar Institution: Slavery in the Ante-bellum South* (New York: Knopf, 1961); and John Hope Franklin, *From Slavery to Freedom* (New York: Knopf, 1961).
2. C. Vann Woodward, *Reunion and Reaction* (Garden City, N.Y.: Doubleday, 1956).

3. C. Vann Woodward, *The Strange Career of Jim Crow* (New York: Oxford University Press, 1957).

4. William Brink and Louis Harris, *The Negro Revolution in America* (New York: Simon and Schuster, 1964), p. 36.

5. Walter White, *A Man Called White* (New York: Viking, 1948), pp. 52 ff.

6. Edmund D. Cronon, *Black Moses* (Madison: University of Wisconsin Press, 1962), pp. 45, 204–207.

7. St. Clair Drake and Horace R. Cayton, *Black Metropolis: A Study of Negro Life in a Northern City* (New York: Harcourt, Brace & World, 1945), pp. 743–744.

8. Herbert Garfinkel, *When Negroes March: The March on Washington Movement in the Organizational Politics for FEPC* (New York: Free Press, 1959).

9. White, *op. cit.*, pp. 143 ff.; and Louis E. Lomax, *The Negro Revolt* (New York: Harper & Row, 1962), pp. 73 ff.

10. Brink and Harris, *op. cit.*, p. 41.

11. Charles E. Silberman, *Crisis in Black and White* (New York: Random House, 1964), pp. 249–307.

12. Lomax, *op. cit.*, p. 73.

13. Martin Luther King, *Stride Toward Freedom: The Montgomery Story* (New York: Harper & Row, 1958).

14. For a sympathetic account of SCLC during its early years, see L. D. Reddick, *Crusader Without Violence: A Biography of Martin Luther King, Jr.* (New York: Harper & Row, 1959), pp. 183 ff. For a more critical discussion, see Lomax, *op. cit.*, pp. 93 ff.

15. Lomax, *op. cit.*, pp. 123–131; Howard Zinn, *The New Abolitionists* (Boston: Beacon Press, 1964), pp. 16–39.

16. Zinn, *op. cit.*, p. 10.

17. James Farmer, *Freedom When?* (New York: Random House, 1965), p. 65. For the early history of CORE see also James Peck, *Freedom Ride* (New York: Simon and Schuster, 1962).

18. Peck, *op. cit.*, pp. 14–27.

19. *Ibid.*, pp. 28–37.

20. *Ibid.*, pp. 38–71.

21. Lomax, *op. cit.*, pp. 135–144.

22. *Ibid.*, pp. 144–145.

23. *Ibid.*

24. Farmer, *op. cit.*, p. 38; and "80 Cafes Integrate in Drive by CORE," *The New York Times*, August 16, 1962, p. 18.

25. Farmer, *op. cit.*, pp. 3–22.

26. *Ibid.*

27. For a complete history of the COFO campaign, see Len Holt, *The Summer That Didn't End* (New York: Morrow, 1965).

28. "A Stillness in Cambridge," *Time*, August 2, 1963, p. 10; and

"Work Demands," *The New York Times,* July 14, 1963, Sec. E, p. 2.

29. "Civil Rights: We Are Dedicated," *Time,* April 17, 1964.

30. "Fair Opens, Rights Stall-In Fails" and "Stall-In Leaders Erred on Backing," *The New York Times,* April 23, 1964, p. 1.

31. Marvin Rich, "The Congress of Racial Equality and Its Strategy," *Annals of the American Academy of Political and Social Science,* 357 (January, 1965), 116.

32. Marvin Rich estimated the percentage of whites among contributors at about 95 percent. Letter from Rich, July 28, 1966.

33. Marvin Rich, "Civil Rights Strategy," *Annals of the American Academy of Political and Social Science,* Vol. 357 (January, 1965). Rich's observations agree with my own during this period.

34. *The New York Times,* July 5, 1964, Sec. 4, p. 1.

35. Thomas Brooks, "The Negro Movement: Beyond Demonstrations," *Dissent,* 12 (Winter, 1965), 16.

CHAPTER 2

Studying the Congress
of Racial Equality

This study is primarily concerned with CORE in the second period of its development: the period of mass direct action. Fieldwork for this study was done during the summers of 1961, 1962, and 1963—the summers of the freedom rides, the freedom highways campaign, the voter registration drive in Mississippi, and the massive demonstrations for fair employment and open housing in Northern cities.

CORE, 1961–1963

In my observations and interviews, I caught CORE in the process of transition from a small, pacifist, predominantly white intellectual group to a more militant, more pragmatic, and less philosophical mass organization in which middle class Negroes and Negro students were replacing whites in positions of influence. My data quite clearly revealed the shift toward a greater emphasis on Negro racial pride, a growing alienation from the white liberal establishment and the white allies of civil rights, and the renunciation of nonviolence as an absolute commitment.

During the period of my study, CORE was also growing rapidly in terms of members, paid staff, and annual budget. In 1960 CORE was a Northern-based organization with fewer than 30 local chapters with a total of about 600 active members and approximately 25,000 financial contributors and operated with a paid staff of four persons. By 1963 the organization had 118 chapters in the North and South with some 6,000 active members, 65,000 financial contributors, and a paid staff of 70 persons, 28 of whom were on permanent, professional-level salaries, the rest being "task force volunteers" on subsistence allowances.[1]

The work of CORE was largely dependent upon, and directed by, the active members of local chapters. The number of such members averaged between twenty-five and fifty per chapter.* These people carried on the day-to-day work of direct action and made policy for the chapter. All projects except national ones were initiated and carried out locally, subject only to adherence to the very general *CORE Rules for Action* (Appendix I). The paid national staff, operating out of New York, was headed by the national director. Under the direction of the New York office, roving and regional field organizers carried out such national projects as the freedom ride and freedom highways projects. In addition, the national office had the major responsibility for organizing new chapters, raising funds for its own operation, supplying funds and legal aid to chapters in need of such help, publicizing the work of CORE on a national level, and putting out a newsletter, *The Corelator*.

According to its constitution, CORE's highest policy-making body was the annual convention, at which all chapters had equal representation. The convention elected a slate of unpaid national officers and a group of regional representatives, who together made up the National Action Council, which made policy decisions between conventions. Actually, CORE's national policy was largely determined by the paid staff members who carried on the day-to-day work of the organization in New York. In this, CORE resembled most large voluntary organizations, with one exception: most decisions and the bulk of the action program were the responsibility of the leaders and active members of local groups.

In addition to the active members of local groups, there was a much larger body of financial contributors, known as associate members, who had no formal voice in running the organization or making its policy, though large contributors undoubtedly exercised considerable informal influence.†

Research Approach

The Congress of Racial Equality was chosen for study because it was the only one of the three direct action groups

* The average number of persons per chapter has increased during the period of this research—1961–1964—from about twenty-five to about fifty.

† In 1963 CORE set up a separate but allied Scholarship, Education, and Defense Fund for Racial Equality, which had the advantage of being authorized to collect tax-deductible contributions for such programs as scholarships for young civil rights workers, voter education, and furnishing of legal counsel to CORE members.

with chapters in the North and South and with a fairly equal proportion of Negro and white members. Within CORE, it was possible to compare Northern and Southern and Negro and white activists. Furthermore, I had already participated in some interregional CORE activities, knew some of the national and local officers, and thus had little difficulty in getting cooperation for my research.

Underlying the choice of research methods was the conviction that meaningful sociological research requires a deep and extensive acquaintance with the subject matter. Several different methods were used. Participant observation was carried out at training institutes, national and regional conventions, and meetings and action projects of all the chapters studied. Some 102 one-page questionnaires (see Appendix II) were filled out by delegates to two national CORE conventions.* Seventy-nine lengthy interviews were carried out with local CORE members and leaders, national staff personnel, and people in the community who had dealt with local groups.

The main body of data was gathered in visits to and interviews with the members of nine local CORE chapters. The five chapters classified as Southern or Border State were in Miami, New Orleans, Baton Rouge, Jackson, and Louisville. The four chapters classified as Northern were in St. Louis, Seattle, Berkeley, and Oakland.† In addition, mem-

* The 1962 midyear winter convention in Cincinnati, Ohio, and the 1962 annual summer convention in Miami, Florida. Some bias was introduced into my sample because it was not possible to get everyone at the convention to fill out a form. Some persons were absent from the sessions at which the questionnaire was administered and others failed to return their form or to fill it out completely. Persons absented themselves from sessions because of lack of interest or responsibility on committees, so that the sample probably lost both little and highly involved delegates. The convention itself is not an accurate reflection of chapter membership since it overrepresents highly active members. Conventions also tend to overrepresent chapters close to the convention site. The fact that we have forms from a Northern and a Southern convention ensures fairly representative geographical distribution.

† The forty groups represented in interviews and questionnaires were divided into Northern, Southern, and Border State chapters as follows: Chapters located in states defined by the United States census as South Atlantic, East South Central, and West South Central were classified as Southern. All other areas except Missouri were classified as Northern. Two Missouri chapters represented a classification problem: St. Louis, which is in an urban environment approximating Northern conditions, and St. Louis County, operating in a small-town environment still largely South-

bers from San Francisco, Los Angeles, and San Jose were interviewed without extended visits to their chapters.

My practice was to spend an average of ten days with each chapter, attending meetings, taking part in direct action, interviewing members and leaders, and participating in the social life of the chapter members. I was greatly aided in this by staying in the homes of CORE members during all but two of my visits. I was thus able to get some insight into the family life of at least one member. I was also able to take part in many informal conversations about CORE and related matters. Also, wherever possible, I interviewed members in their homes in order to obtain further insight into their lives.

In all these contacts, I told the persons under study that I was working on a sociological dissertation on CORE, and generally I was not asked to describe the research more closely than this. However, since I was also known to some members of the groups under observation as a member of a local group and a past participant in a national project, I was more frequently accepted as a fellow CORE member, especially by those persons to whom the research was not particularly understandable or meaningful. The personal contacts made and the generous hospitality and cooperation shown by so many members reflected the intensely close bonds that tied CORE members together. As a visiting CORE member, I was automatically entitled to the warmest and most informal hospitality and help.

The type of acceptance that I was accorded as a fellow CORE member helped greatly to break down barriers between myself and the respondents. Among many Southern Negroes, whites fall into two very distinct categories: outsiders, who are generally enemies; and white CORE members, who are put into an entirely different category and granted considerable confidence. I believe that the main bias operating in my interviews with Negroes was their unwillingness to criticize white persons within the movement, people whom they interpreted as being like me. The full extent of hostility against whites in general was probably somewhat muted, but I noticed no great unwillingness to express themselves on this topic.

As for the white respondents, rapport was usually very

----

ern in character. I decided to classify these chapters by the social situation: St. Louis CORE as Northern and St. Louis County CORE as Southern.

easy since most of them move in a milieu similar to my own. One probable source of bias in *these* interviews, however, is that whites in CORE tend to be more militant around Negroes than around other whites. It is probable, therefore, that whites would have expressed greater militancy and radicalism to a Negro interviewer than to me, and this greater militancy might have reflected more correctly their conduct in CORE groups, where Negroes are always present.

The interviews averaged two and a half hours in length. Except for a short list of specific questions about social background that repeated the questions asked in the written questionnaire, these interviews were loosely structured. They followed a very general interviewing guide that sought to lead the respondent over several major areas: social background, motives for joining the movement, attitudes toward the goals of the movement and time perspective on the movement, experiences in the movement, attitudes toward nonviolence, attitudes toward the race problem, attitudes toward the social system in general, and attitudes toward the internal problems of the CORE chapter. Officers and staff members were asked additional questions about the past history and current projects of their group (see Appendixes III and IV).

During these interviews I permitted respondents to veer away from the scheduled subjects for considerable periods of time, for it was my purpose to discover what things were prominent in their lives and thinking. Respondents seldom wandered completely off the subject of CORE, which was almost always their most compelling current interest. I found that many of the rules I had learned about scientifically correct interviewing had to be discarded. The cool, nonresponsive, "neutrally probing" interviewer is, I now believe, only successful with populations trained to be cooperative respondents. Many of my respondents reacted to such a stance with alarm and unwillingness to express themselves. I found it necessary to talk to them as one person to another, exchanging ideas, experiences, and emotional reactions. In this type of give-and-take dialogue one runs the risk of biasing the responses by indicating one's own views, and the interviewer must remain ever alert to that danger. But on the whole, I do not consider bias to be as crucial a problem as getting a full and lively response.

In my forty-six interviews with members, I aimed for coverage that would reflect the social make-up of the chapter. No rigid sampling method could be used because membership lists were not always up-to-date and were sometimes not available owing to the general atmosphere of suspicion and fear of local reprisals. My method was first to get as complete a description of active members as possible from a local officer and then to select respondents who reflected the different social types in the chapter. Although I made some effort not to limit myself to very active, vocal people, the sample is surely skewed in that direction. The breakdown of the forty-six interviews by race and region was as follows:

SOUTH		NORTH	
Negro	*White*	*Negro*	*White*
16	7	12	11

In addition to interviews with CORE members and leaders, fifteen interviews were with persons in the community who had come in contact with CORE in their capacity as leaders of other civil rights groups or as businessmen who had been under attack by CORE.

Commitment and Bias

It is essential in a work of this kind to discuss the problem of commitment and bias. It is my profound conviction that there is no unbiased vantage point from which the social scientist can view a controversial social problem. Because we can never fully know every aspect of a situation, each particular approach represents some distortion of reality. Yet there obviously are degrees of approximation toward objectivity. With reference to any single group, movement, or institution, objectivity can be increased if the investigator undergoes the process of viewing the group from the vantage point of various other groups in society. I use the term "undergo" advisedly here because I do not believe that the process of grasping different perspectives can be a purely cerebral one. It requires real immersion in the emotions and experiences of the various groups that serve as vantage points. Yet, because the time of the investigator is always limited, he must to some extent choose between the gaining of many outsiders' perspectives and the attainment of one intimate and detailed insider's perspective.

My choice lay very clearly on the side of intimate, insider's knowledge, partly because of my preference for studying a limited subject intensively and partly because of my personal commitment to the civil rights movement and to CORE. The commitment came into being at the same time the research was begun and increased steadily. For three years I participated actively in the work of my local chapter and region. During these years my closest friends were those who shared my involvement in the movement; at the same time I was carrying on the research, I underwent much of the process of socialization described in my chapter on the white members of CORE. Even more than the average CORE member, I found myself immersed in the outlook of the Negro members and preoccupied with the philosophical problems and political issues confronting the movement.

During the course of the research, I found myself deeply attracted to the philosophy of nonviolence—something that is not so typical of active participants. Unable to accept this view completely, however, I was caught between the ethics of political responsibility for the end results of one's actions and the absolutist commitment to nonviolent means that came to me through the writings of Gandhi and the Quakers. If I "debunked" the direct actionists' commitment to nonviolence, it was not as an enemy of that philosophy but rather as a disappointed, though not wholly consistent, lover of that philosophy. Indeed, the disappointment of discovering that the direct actionists had a shallow view of nonviolence deepened into a disappointment with reality. For, as I carried out the research for this book and simultaneously became actively engaged in the movement, I came to realize the overwhelming importance of coercion in human affairs. Nowhere did this point come home more vividly than when, in my analysis of the social and psychological underpinnings of the commitment to nonviolence, I found nonviolence to be the fruit of psychological and political weakness: an enormously appealing moral viewpoint brought about by coercive conditions and bound to disappear when those conditions changed. Yet I found it impossible to carry these realizations to their logical conclusion. On the contrary, I developed, through my contacts, a more profound appreciation of the qualities of humility and generosity, which characterized many of the most nonviolent persons in the movement. In the face of coercive society, one cannot help but love the meek, not because they will inherit the earth—they will not—but because they are gentle and do not despoil it.

Organization of the Study

The study begins with an analysis of CORE's ideology as expressed in publications and by spokesmen of the nonviolent direct action movement inside and outside CORE during the period of mass direct action. Next it explores the ideological influences that impinged on CORE during this period: those pulling for greater militance and those pulling for greater moderation.

Chapter 5 describes the social backgrounds and current social positions of the active CORE members. Here we try to see what types, Negro and white, Northern and Southern, join the ranks of a militant direct action movement. Chapter 6 describes the organization and strategy of a typical Southern CORE chapter as it relates to, or fights against, various elements within the Negro and white communities and explains how and why the direct action strategy works to bring about social change.

Chapter 7 explores the ideology of rank-and-file Negro members: what nonviolence means to them in the context of their general viewpoint. Looking again at the same group of Negro members, Chapter 8 addresses itself to who are the radicals, who are the moderates, and what is the nature and meaning of radicalism and moderation within the context of CORE ideology and strategy. Chapter 9 looks at the white CORE members' ideological development as they are drawn into CORE and come under the influence of the Negro activists' outlook.

Following the conclusion, the Epilogue describes and analyzes the major changes in CORE philosophy and strategy that emerged during the period of ghetto organization after 1964. Here we find the end of the commitment to nonviolence, which is a major concern throughout the book. The reasons for this important change and for the various radicalizing trends that accompanied it are explored throughout the entire study. If the book had been completed in 1963, it would have included, on the basis of the findings, a prediction of the imminent breakdown of the nonviolent philosophy. Events moved more quickly than the slow processes of scholarship, and this study is now not a basis for prediction but an analysis that provides some explanation of what happened to nonviolence in the direct action movement.

NOTE

1. *The New York Times*, August 10, 1964, p. 16.

CHAPTER 3

Pacifism and the Direct Action Movement

Appeal from Tyranny to the Constitution

The Congress of Racial Equality, like all civil rights groups in American history, has developed very little new ideology in the area of goals or in the nature of the desired society. In examining the newsletters and pamphlets issued by CORE, one is immediately struck by the fact that most of them are devoted to fairly straightforward accounts of direct action campaigns. Rarely does one find in these documents any broad economic, political, or sociological analysis or critique of American society. Unlike the ideology of many radical movements, such as the French Revolution or the Marxist labor movement, here there was no systematic attack on the official values of society, nor was there any attempt to substitute another world view or a new utopian vision. From the beginning, the movement did not focus its ideology in these directions because it relied almost wholly on the Constitution and the official "American creed" of human equality. The importance of this creed and the extent to which it conflicts with the reality of the Negro's status is clearly spelled out by Gunnar Myrdal in his historic study of the American race problem. Myrdal summarized the creed:

> These ideals of the essential dignity of the individual human being, of the fundamental equality of all men, and of certain inalienable rights to freedom, justice, and a fair opportunity . . . these tenets were written into the Declaration of Independence, the Preamble of the Constitution, the Bill of Rights and into the constitutions of the several states. The ideals of the American Creed have thus become the highest law of the land.[1]

The creed itself was enough to condemn discrimination, and its realization via enforcement of the Constitution was the goal of the movement.

Since most of CORE's propaganda was directed toward Negroes and Northern white liberals—its potential activists and financial supporters—there was no need for any fundamental philosophical discussion of the goal of equality. The assumption underlying CORE's propaganda style was clearly that its audience was sufficiently committed to the American creed and that they only needed to have the contrast between the real and the ideal made dramatic enough to justify drastic action and to call forth strong commitments. In the words of one pamphleteer:

> How do we make a situation real to outsiders—those who know not the people involved, the state, the county, and most of all, the social, political, economic, cultural, religious, and historical pattern we have labelled "segregation."
> This report is intended to make facts real and evoke not reader interest but productive commitments. The method need not be demagoguery however, just read the facts. And read them again. And again.[2]

The typical "account" dealt with a civil rights campaign in the South. The opening scene revealed the poverty of the local Negro community, their exclusion from the polls, and the indignities that were part of their everyday lives. This was followed by a description of a voter registration drive or sit-in campaign with carefully chronicled accounts of police brutality, injustice in the local courts, mob violence, economic intimidation, and expression of racist sentiments by local leaders and newspapers. Sometimes the discrepancy between the ideal and the real was explicitly underlined through irony, as in one pamphlet that told about injustice against integrationists in Louisiana courts and had on its cover the blindfolded figure holding the scales, with the bold lettering "JUSTICE?" written across her picture. A pamphlet on the same subject had an American shield and eagle on the front with the caption "It happened in Baton Rouge, U.S.A." Another booklet, describing a violence-ridden campaign in Danville, Virginia, gave a straightforward account of conditions and events, and each paragraph was introduced by a particularly apt quotation from the Danville Chamber of Commerce on the pleasantness of the city. Sometimes the conclusions were drawn explicitly and strongly, as in the following introduction to the reprint of an article on the criminal-anarchy indictment of Negro leaders in Baton Rouge:

One has to search the repressive codes of the most loathsome Communist and Fascist tyrannies to match Louisiana's latest device for trying to curb the integrationist movement. This is to charge active advocates of civil rights who run afoul of the law with "criminal anarchy." Conviction under this charge means a 10–30 year sentence on the chain gang.[3]

The comparison between Southern conditions and the conditions in totalitarian and fascist countries was made frequently and was both an appeal to American values and an attempt to justify what might seem to be an extreme and overly dramatic response. Thus, one pamphleteer closed his account of violence and arrests in McComb by quoting words written by Ignazio Silone about Italian fascism: "No word and no gesture can be more persuasive than the life, and if necessary the death, of a man who strives to be free . . . a man who shows what a man can be." And the author added: "Extreme words, these. But the time for man has come." [4]

In a similar vein, Martin Luther King legitimated the aspirations of his followers by calling on the symbols and examples of American history. Of the young direct actionists, he said:

> These young people have connected up with their own history —the slave revolts, the incomplete revolution of the Civil War, the brotherhood of colonial colored men in Africa and Asia. They are an integral part of the history which is reshaping the world, replacing a dying order with modern democracy. They are doing this in a nation whose own birth spread new principles and shattered a medieval society then dominating most of the globe.[5]

Referring to the signers of the Declaration of Independence, forced to struggle against the abuses of the British crown, he said, "The Negro students, their parents, and their allies are acting today in that imperishable tradition." [6]

The federal government was generally treated rather kindly in these propaganda materials. Federal court decisions reversing state court decisions as well as intervention by the FBI and Civil Rights Commission substantiated the claim that this was a struggle between the Constitution and local dictatorships. Occasionally, however, federal agencies came in for open criticism. A pamphlet reporting the findings of a "Committee of Inquiry into Southern Justice" opened with a statement by Norman Thomas, in which, after summarizing the committee's evidence on police intimidation, violence, and judicial discrimination, he concluded, "In these stories the federal power is often inaccessible. Frequently men of the FBI, though present, might as well not have been." [7]

Off the record, leaders were often outspokenly bitter about the federal government, particularly the Justice Department and the FBI. In 1962 James Farmer, speaking informally to a group of Northern CORE members, summed up the situation with regard to federal protection as follows:

> We had a meeting recently in Washington, D.C., between the Department of Justice and those organizations working on voter registration. The workers from the South asked the Justice Department for protection, especially in Mississippi and Georgia. The Department refused. We asked them to send *even one Marshal* when we are bringing people into courthouses where we know they will be intimidated. The answer was no. The Department had promised us protection on voter registration whereas, so they told us, they couldn't help us on sit-ins or Freedom Rides, and things like that. They often say they cannot prove violence is directly related to voter registration, as when a church is burned in which people were being trained. They tell us that they are bound by statutory limitation—but we know from past experience that when the heat is on these limitations are gotten around very fast. We have to continue to create crises like the Freedom Rides, in order to get them to act.[8]

We shall see in later chapters that the "insiders" in CORE condemned the entire liberal establishment as one that had to be pushed toward every inch of civil rights progress, but this disaffection was usually confined to the policies and motives of the country's leaders. It did not extend to a general disillusionment with the democratic-constitutional structure of government.

Roots of the Nonviolent Philosophy

In contrast with the absence of ideology in the area of goals, the direct action movement developed an elaborate ideology of means. The philosophy of nonviolence brought a new and essentially alien viewpoint into American politics. In attempting such an innovation, the movement was diverging markedly from the pragmatic, nonideological character of most American social movements.

Most of the early CORE members were principled pacifists, inspired by Quaker philosophy and the writings of Gandhi. For twelve years before Martin Luther King appeared on the American scene, small dedicated groups of CORE members were applying nonviolent direct action to the problem of segregation. Yet CORE developed only the most pragmatic and minimal elaborations on the basic idea of nonviolence; the organization never produced an outstanding ideological spokesman. The fact that it was King, and not CORE—well supplied as it was with intellectuals and long-time pacifists— who really elaborated and applied the philosophy of non- violence to the integration struggle was undoubtedly due to the fact that he was the first leader who tried to justify massive resistance in the Deep South. CORE's actions until 1954 took place entirely in the North and upper South and never in- volved large numbers of people. In these situations the mere practice of courtesy, patience, and nonretaliation appears to have served as sufficient legitimation for the relatively small amounts of coercion that the isolated CORE groups were able to bring on businessmen. After 1961, when CORE began to engage in large-scale campaigns in the South and North, it relied heavily on Martin Luther King for its ideology. King's writings were familiar to all CORE members. When CORE appealed to a wide public for support of its campaigns, it depended for its ideological context on the nonviolent doctrine that King had developed and presented to the American pub- lic. In the following pages we shall look briefly at the Quaker and Gandhian sources on which both CORE and King drew and that King, in particular, modified and developed to fit the needs of the American integration movement.

In Gandhi's philosophy, nonviolence—not just noninjury, but positive goodwill toward the evildoer—was the indispen- sable cornerstone of ethical action. Nonviolence was not just a means to other ends, it was itself the highest end, and all other goals were subordinate to it. There was no desirable political goal that would not be compromised and distorted were violence used to attain it. Gandhi counseled his followers that if they perfected their means, desirable ends would inevitably follow.[9]

This absolute commitment to nonviolent means originated in a religious framework. Indifference to specific goals was based on the traditional Hindu teaching that wisdom is found in a progressive detachment from all desire for things of this world. Gandhi's emphasis on nonpossession, renunciation of sensual pleasure, discipline of the senses, and the positive virtue of suffering was part of this concern with attaining a state of detachment from the world.[10] It is only in the light of this essentially religious "antiworldly" orientation toward political action that we can fully understand the renunciation of ends as well as the absolute perfection of means in Gandhi's doctrine of nonviolence.

Gandhi distinguished sharply between his nonviolent movement, *Satyagraha* (best translated as "truth seeking"), and passive resistance, *Duragraha,* as practiced by the suffragettes and other Western movements. Passive resistance, he said, is used by those who are interested in a specific goal but are too weak to use violence to attain it. The weakness might be purely physical or it might be psychological, such as insufficient courage. In passive resistance, violence is not renounced on principle, nor is nonviolence adopted as the overriding principle that is the central and inseparable part of the movement's goal. Here nonviolence arises out of a temporary condition and is often used while preparing for violence or side by side with it.[11]

Satyagraha, by contrast, is first and foremost a weapon of the strong. Only those can practice it who have, at least on a psychological level, the strength to fight violently, because fighting through self-suffering requires greater courage than fighting violently. *Satyagraha* is based on the realization that nonviolence is the pivotal principle and all others are secondary to it. Without the attainment of this conviction and thus this superior strength, a movement will give up its passive resistance the moment it becomes strong enough to use violent means. One crucial aspect of Gandhi's thought is that when the only choice is between cowardice and violence, violence is preferable. He ranked passive resistance below violent resistance; true nonviolence, of course, was the highest moral form.

The second major source of nonviolent philosophy was the tradition of Christian pacifism, practiced most notably in modern times by the Quakers. The Quaker sect was one of many mystic, Christian-perfectionist sects that emerged in Europe during the seventeenth century. All these groups were intensely otherworldly and advocated noninvolvement in politics and nonresistance to force. Although in most sects this doctrine led to a complete retreat from political involvement, the Quakers translated their opposition to violence into practical action first in their peaceful relations with the Indians in the colony of Pennsylvania and then in social movements like abolitionism and prison reform. During the twentieth century, the Quakers extended their antiwar position into active campaigns for medical service on the war fronts and relief for war-damaged nations.[12]

The cornerstone of Quaker theology was the assertion that "there is a seed of God in every soul." [13] This tenet served to make the individual, whose revelation comes directly from God, the center of religious life and authority. The clergy, the doctrines and sacraments of the church, and even the absolute authority of the Biblical text were put aside in favor of individual revelation. Quaker philosophy, with its emphasis on the quality of individuals rather than on the importance of groups, institutions, or doctrines, strongly influenced the modern peace movement. In assessing the world situation, the Quaker began with the recognition that all governments, all ideologies, and all symbols were meaningless when compared with the importance of the quality of individual lives. The labels "good" and "evil" could not be applied to nations or doctrines, because both conditions existed among the "enemy" as well as within one's own camp.[14] "Goodness" was equated with nonviolence and positive love for others. As in Gandhian philosophy, nonviolence was not a means to some other end but was itself the one and only healing power and the central goal of the Quaker's action. Just as in Gandhi's philosophy the overriding emphasis on means was buttressed by the doctrine of detachment from the fruits of action, so in Quaker thought was adherence to nonviolence, regardless of the consequences, supported by an underlying attitude of otherworldliness.

Both Quaker and Gandhian thought used nonviolence as the basis of a radical critique of existing society. Gandhi's philosophy led him to confront not only British power in India but also ancient Indian aspects of the caste system. For the Quakers, nonviolence called into question all militarism, all racial and class differences, and much in the exercise of governmental power. In this sense, the two philosophies not only were absolutist with regard to nonviolence but also were expressistic of a particular type of ideological radicalism.

Nonviolence as a Legitimation of Direct Action

Martin Luther King chose the doctrine of nonviolence for use within a movement that was intensely concerned with one specific goal: equal rights for the Negro. In his philosophical pronouncements, he mixed absolutist support for nonviolence with pragmatic arguments that pointed to the numerical weakness of the Negroes—making violence impractical.[15] Nowhere in King's thinking do we find Gandhi's differentiation between passive resistance and nonviolence or Gandhi's purist insistence that nonviolence must be the weapon of the strong, whereas violence is preferable to cowardice for the weak. Nor did King ever examine the means-ends problem in any depth. The possibility that nonviolent means might not always be the best or only way to attain the goal of civil rights was never discussed in his writings or speeches. His followers were never confronted with the possibility that they might have to make a choice between their end and the nonviolent means, nor were they given any systematic doctrine of means and ends that could predispose them to renounce the end in favor of the means, should a practical choice arise.

This ambivalence with regard to nonviolent absolutism was not surprising, given the absence of general religious or cultural support for such a doctrine in American society. Yet Martin Luther King's message had an immediate and broad appeal to direct action groups and their sympathizers. Why? Why could the movement not have been openly pragmatic in using nonviolence as a necessary tactic? Why did it not continue in the tradition of the American labor movement, which used direct action but never renounced the right of self-defense? The answers lie in the fact that the Negro's claim to equality and his right to use strong methods to attain it were so widely questioned by the prevailing culture that even the members of the movement had to legitimate their activity in their own eyes by denying the extent of the coercion they used and by renouncing the right of self-defense. Thus, it was claimed that through the example of voluntary suffering and constant kindness and forbearance the conscience of the enemy would eventually be touched and he would be converted to friendship and reconciled to integration.[16] The tension and suffering inherent in the process of social change were, it was claimed, borne by the Negro. In promoting boycotts, the Negro community was not putting on pressure but withdrawing cooperation and willingly bearing all the trouble that came with such a withdrawal. The image of the old Negro servant walking many miles to work during the Montgomery bus boycott was the typical symbol of this version of the nonviolent strategy.

> We will match your capacity to inflict suffering with our capacity to endure suffering. We will meet your physical force with soul force. We will not hate you, but we cannot in all good conscience obey your unjust laws. Do to us what you will and we will still love you. Bomb our homes and threaten our children; send your hooded perpetrators of violence into our communities and drag us out on some wayside road, beating us and leaving us half dead, and we will still love you. But we will soon wear you down by our capacity to suffer. And in winning our freedom we will so appeal to your heart and conscience that we will win you in the process.[17]

This statement expresses an essentially unrealistic version of how nonviolent direct action brought about social change. In reality, the strategy worked by putting economic pressure on businessmen and political pressure on politicians. The conversion of businessmen and politicians through the moral power of nonviolence was so rare as to be insignificant. Leaders of direct action groups knew this and planned their campaigns accordingly. Yet these same leaders usually expressed, and half believed, the "official" version of nonviolence.

The nonviolent doctrine also added legitimacy to the Negro's drive for power by making him the bearer of the great message of nonviolence, his destiny to redeem the American white man from racism and the world from the violence of war: "It may even be possible for the Negro, through adherence to non-violence, so to challenge the nations of the world that they will seriously seek an alternative to war and destruction . . ." [18]

Such glorifications countered the prevailing doubts about the Negro's human equality with claims to his moral superiority. As Bertrand Russell pointed out in his essay "The Superior Virtue of the Oppressed," [19] all movements in behalf of oppressed groups have found it necessary to claim moral superiority for their constituents in order to justify their having the same rights as everybody else. This movement was certainly as much in need of such undergirding as any comparable movement in Western history.

The doctrine of nonviolence also reconciled Negro participants to a stance that the culture as a whole considered weak. If nonviolence were interpreted as merely a tactic necessitated by weakness, there would be a constant sense of frustration and impotence. However, by making nonviolence an end in itself and by making the Negro's mission not merely the attainment of equality but the introduction of a new moral standard into American political life, the doctrine attempted to change what might have been a sense of impotence into a sense of superiority. The demonstrator who went to jail wearing a lapel pin that said, "Father forgive them," was surely elevated by the inner knowledge that the end of that quotation, applied here to the whites, read, "for they know not what they do." King was sometimes very clear in calling upon the Negro to transform his actual weakness into a sense of moral strength:

> . . . I pray that, recognizing the necessity of suffering, the Negro will make of it a virtue. To suffer in a righteous cause is to grow to our humanity's full stature. If only to save himself from bitterness, the Negro needs the vision to see the ordeals of this generation as the opportunity to transfigure himself and American society . . .[20]

Exoteric and Esoteric Ideology in CORE

I have suggested that, in the civil rights movement, the doctrine of nonviolence was mainly a way of legitimating direct action in a society that doubted the Negro's claim to equality. If this hypothesis is correct, one might expect to find in the examination of CORE's ideology that the emphasis on nonviolence decreases as one moves from the exoteric communications of CORE—those beamed to potential supporters outside the organization—to the esoteric communications—those directed to the active members.* The insiders, being solidly convinced of the legitimacy of the goal of equality, should be more willing to accept coercion as a means to that

* The terms "exoteric" and "esoteric" are taken from Gabriel Almond, *The Appeals of Communism* (Princeton, N.J.: Princeton University Press, 1954). In his analysis of Communist party communications, Almond used these terms to differentiate between the content of communications geared to outsiders and those directed at insiders. The differentiation is useful, even though one may reject Almond's implication that the Communist party is peculiar in having markedly different exoteric and esoteric messages. This difference undoubtedly characterizes all political groups, though the extent of the divergence varies and probably depends on the degree to which the esoteric ideology is considered illegitimate in the larger society.

end. Being more certain of the Negro's basic right to equality, they should be less prone to demand the moral superiority of renouncing the right of self-defense. The following comparison of exoteric and esoteric CORE communications bears out this expectation.

During the period of this study, CORE's printed literature was directed mainly to the Northern white liberals who made up the bulk of the organization's financial supporters.* The ideological climate of this audience was reflected in various features of the literature. Although CORE depended on the writings of Martin Luther King for its general ideological foundation and although the emphasis was on winning over the enemy through persuasion and goodwill, the literature was markedly lacking in religious argument or in extended philosophical discussion of nonviolence. The white liberal audience was not predominantly religious, nor was it interested in nonviolence as a radical new ideology. All that was required of practitioners of nonviolence was that they make direct action tactics palatable by promising to avoid serious disruption of public order and naked coercion of whites.

CORE's largest pamphlet, Cracking the Color Line,[21] described several Northern campaigns conducted against restaurants and amusement facilities in the 1940s and 1950s. Careful preliminary "testing" that established the existence of discrimination was described. This period was followed by a negotiation phase, involving many months of patient attempts to persuade businessmen to change their policies. The discipline, orderliness, and goodwill of the demonstrators were described. The accounts stressed the widespread support that the demonstrations gained from white patrons, policemen, and onlookers; the relative ease with which integration was accepted once it was attained; and the unreality of businessmen's fears about losing customers and white employees. Segregation was made to sound like a shallow-rooted hangover from the past that gave way like melting snow before the firm but patient assault of small, dedicated CORE groups.

A more emotional pamphlet, Jailed-In (1961), by field secretary Thomas Gaither, gave a moving account of the effectiveness of nonviolence in a Southern prison. The writer

* Marvin Rich, former program director of national CORE, estimated that 95 percent of the financial contributors were white. This audience is also the group from which most white activists were recruited. (Letter from M. Rich, July, 1966.)

described how the decision of the demonstrators to accept jail rather than pay bail "disarmed" the Southern whites and caused consternation in the courtroom. The author described the brutality of authorities in jail; he also revealed the power of nonviolent goodwill in winning over the white prisoners who had initially been hostile. One of these prisoners was moved to write to the FBI to complain of the unjust treatment of the civil rights prisoners, and many whites asked the Negro protesters to entertain them by singing their freedom songs.

The version of nonviolent direct action and white response given in these pamphlets was in line with the white liberal's view of racism as a passing anachronism within American democracy. The real villain, when he appeared in CORE literature, was also the villain of the liberal ideology: the Deep South racist—usually a low class hoodlum or local "redneck" sheriff. In these accounts, pathos and heroism were derived from the dramatic contrast between the behavior and attitudes of the segregationists and those of the nonviolent resisters. The following description of violence in McComb, Mississippi, illustrates this contrast. It also provides a good example of the picture of Southern reality given in most accounts:

(The author and his associates are standing in front of the McComb courthouse after having brought Negroes down to register. A member of a white mob that had gathered approached and asked:) "Boy, what's your business?" at which point I knew I was in trouble. The clerk from the hallway came to the back door leading to the courthouse with a smile on his face and called to the white man, "Wait a minute; wait a minute!" At this point the white man, whom they called Bryant, hit me in my right eye. Then I saw this clerk motion his head as if to call the rest of the whites. They came and all circled around me, and this fellow that was called Bryant hit me on my jaw, then on my chin. Then he slammed me down; instead of falling, I stumbled onto the courthouse lawn. The crowd (about 15, I think) followed, making comments. He was holding me so tight around the collar; I put my hands on the collar to ease the choking. The clerk hollered, "Why don't you hit him back?" This set off a reaction of punches from this fellow they called Bryant; I counted fifteen; he just kept hitting and shouting. "Yes, why don't you hit me, nigger? Yes, why don't you hit me, nigger?" I was beaten into a semi-conscious state. My vision was blurred by the punch in the eye. I heard Bob tell me to cover my head to avoid any further blows to the face. I told Bryant if he was through beating me, I was ready to go. The clerk said, yes I should go. Then this guy they called

Bryant yelled, "Brothers, shall we kill him here?" I was extremely frightened by the sincere way he said it. No one in the crowd answered the question, and Bryant . . . released me. Moses then took me by the arm and took me to the street, walking cautiously to avoid any further kicks or blows. The Negro fellow that had been taking the registration test gave up in the excitement, and we saw him in his truck, the white men advised him to get the hell out of town, saying they were surprised that he was associating with our kind. Charges were not pressed.[22]

Most of this literature was aimed at liberal white audiences, so there was no attempt to urge the reader to accept non-violence and to discipline himself in its techniques. It was, rather, a legitimation of direct action and a play for sympathy and commitment from a group that might be only mildly well disposed and was certainly in no danger of breaking out into violence over the issue. The possible abandonment of non-violence was, indeed, sometimes used as a veiled threat against those who did not help the movement progress fast enough:

In other countries [freedom] is being achieved by violence. In America there is still a chance that it can be achieved peacefully. We white people cannot be grateful enough that men like Martin Luther King, with their emphasis on non-violence, are still the leaders of Southern Negroes. For the rise in power of other Negro forces (such as the Black Muslims) makes clear that it may soon be too late to achieve integration by non-violent means.[23]

In contrast to the emphasis on nonviolent persuasion in the esoteric CORE literature, the insider gradually learned a viewpoint that was more frankly favorable to the use of coercion. The person who joined a chapter as an active member or became acquainted with CORE by attending one of the annual summer training institutes run by the national CORE office* was usually introduced to CORE by a small pamphlet, *CORE Rules for Action* (Appendix I), used throughout the organization during this period as a basic document on CORE

* Some of the observations in this section are taken from participant observation at one such training institute held in Alexandria, Virginia. The institute was led by six members of the national staff and attended by forty persons from all over the country. It lasted for three weeks during August, 1961. Two such training institutes, one in the South and one in the North, are held every summer. They generally last from one to three weeks.

tactics. In its introductory section, the leaflet summarizes the official goals and methods of the organization:

> The nonviolent direct action approach to problems of racial discrimination assumes that a lasting resolution of problems can best be obtained through a spirit of good will and understanding. This spirit must be combined with a determination to end discrimination through action programs directed to specific problems. The ultimate goal is an integrated society where each member is judged solely on the basis of his individual worth.

The leaflet then outlines rules of conduct that require CORE members to always know and be able to prove the facts in any given case, to attempt to understand the position and attitudes of all sides, and to make a "sincere effort to avoid malice and hatred toward any group or individual." Other items deal with group discipline, pointing out that members can dissent from any proposed action and refuse to participate on the basis of dissent. When in a project, however, members should obey the orders of the leadership and should not withdraw unless they no longer feel able to adhere to the rules of nonviolence.

In local groups and at training institutes, leaders might sometimes give a traditional Gandhian interpretation of nonviolence, stressing the importance of self-sacrifice and good-will in changing the hearts and minds of segregationists. Yet it was made clear that these were private views, and though it might be implied that such attitudes represent the highest ethical standard, it was also explicitly stated that CORE did not expect its members to make absolutist or all-embracing personal commitments to nonviolence. The new member was given to understand that it was sufficient for him to commit himself to nonviolence on CORE projects only. There was generally very little soul searching on the score of inner attitudes. Nonviolence was supported by most members as the only practical tactic to be used in the South. The discussion of nonviolence was carried on in a predominantly secular context.

The major emphasis was on practical techniques of direct action. The standard "steps" of testing, negotiating, publicizing and building community support, picketing, sitting-in, and going to jail were carefully discussed and often worked through in sociodramas. There was considerable emphasis on carrying out these procedures in a polite and "professional" manner. But despite the stress on politeness, the group was developing a strategy designed to maximize coercion, short of physical violence or verbal abuse. In sessions on employment projects, for example, there was careful consideration of the types of firms that could be most easily pressured by boycotts and the times of year when stores would be most vulnerable to picketing. In discussions of arrest, the emphasis was on such practical items as getting the officer's badge number, knowing the charges before submitting to arrest, and contacting a lawyer once in jail. The new member who wanted to discuss his inner loves and hates or the possibility of reaching the opponent's heart was made to feel that he was off the track. Underlying most discussions was the clear assumption that efficiency in bringing maximum economic pressure was the only way to attain results.

Summary

In the area of goals, the civil rights movement never developed an elaborate ideology, because it was simply concerned with the inclusion of the Negro in American society. Because the official "American creed" supported this ambition, it was unnecessary to develop any elaborate new ideology to buttress the Negro's aspirations.

The direct action movement that emerged in the late 1950s and early 1960s made no new ideological departures in this area either. It did, however, develop an elaborate ideology in the area of means: the philosophy of nonviolence that was borrowed from the absolutist, otherworldly philosophies of Gandhi and the Quakers. The main function of this philosophy in the civil rights movement was to make the new direct action tactics legitimate in the eyes of the public and among members of the movement.

There are two reasons why this tactic required strong and elaborate legitimation. First, although direct action had been practiced by other American movements and some methods, like the strike, had gained considerable public acceptance, most instances of direct action, especially those types involving civil disobedience, were still considered illegitimate by the public. This alone would hardly explain an emphasis on nonviolence that went so far as to deny the element of coercion and to forbid self-defense. The labor movement, which pioneered in the use of direct action and civil disobedience, never went in for such legitimation.

The second and more compelling need for legitimation arose from the gap between official creed and unofficial belief on the question of race, in the depths of the "American dilemma." Doubts about the Negro's right to equality were reflected by doubts about the legitimacy of using strong means for attaining this end. Moreover, as we have seen, CORE literature that had to appeal to the less-involved and less-committed sympathizers stressed nonviolence and played down the element of coercion involved in direct action. To argue that nonviolence was necessary to the movement because it won allies among Northern white liberals is another way of saying that the justice of the Negro's claim was not fully accepted by many potential and actual supporters.* Among the active "insiders," on the other hand, nonviolence was adopted mainly as a tactic, and concern for conversion through goodwill gave way to open support for economic coercion as the only way of attaining practical results.

NOTES

1. Gunnar Myrdal, *An American Dilemma* (New York: McGraw-Hill, 1964), p. 4.
2. Tom Hayden, *Revolution in Mississippi* (New York: Students

* Some observers have explained adherence to nonviolence by pointing to the "obvious futility" of the use of violence by an outnumbered group. How "obvious" this is, however, depends on one's fundamental ideological assumptions. There have been occasions on which violence brought more progress than had previously been achieved by other means. The Harlem riot of August, 1943, for example, led to the organization of the first local committee to open jobs to Negroes. (See Walter White, *A Man Called White* [New York: Viking, 1948], pp. 233–241.) Those who support the Negro's right to use self-defense argue that armed defense organizations have cut down white violence in Monroe, North Carolina, Bogalusa, Louisiana, and other areas. It is impossible to judge these claims without further evidence. What is obvious, however, is that the "obvious futility" argument rests on emotional appeal rather than systematic evidence.

The "obvious futility" argument actually supports the hypothesis put forth in this chapter, because the reason violence might cause a "backlash" against Negroes is precisely that their right to equality is not widely accepted. The right of Jews to attack Nazi party demonstrators, for example, is generally accepted, and no dire consequences have resulted from such incidents, even though Jews constitute a tiny minority.

for a Democratic Society, 1962), p. 5. (Pamphlet circulated by CORE and SNCC.)

3. Introduction to reprint of a column by Murray Kempton, "The Trial," *New York Post*, March 21, 1962. (Circulated by CORE.)
4. Hayden, *op. cit.*, p. 28.
5. Martin Luther King, "The Burning Truth in the South," *The Progressive*, Madison, 1960. (Reprint circulated by SCLC.)
6. *Ibid.*
7. Charlotte Devree, ed., *Justice* (New York: CORE, ca. 1962).
8. Meeting between James Farmer and Bay Area CORE leaders and members, Berkeley, October, 1962.
9. M. K. Gandhi, *The Story of My Experiments with Truth* (Washington, D.C.: Public Affairs Press, 1948); and M. K. Gandhi, *Satyagraha in South Africa* (Triplicane, Madras: S. Ganesan, 1928). For an excellent discussion of Gandhi's philosophy, see John V. Bondurant, *Conquest of Violence* (Princeton, N.J.: Princeton University Press, 1958).
10. For some of the religious background of Gandhi's philosophy, see S. Radhakrishnan, *The Bhagavadgita* (London: Allen, 1948).
11. Lee Kuper, *Passive Resistance in South Africa* (New Haven: Yale University Press, 1957), p. 74.
12. G. W. Knowles, *Quakers and Peace*, The Grotius Society Publications, No. 4 (London: Sweet & Maxwell, 1927); and Rufus M. Jones, *The Faith and Practice of the Quakers* (London: Methuen, n.d.).
13. Jones, *op. cit.*, p. 28.
14. *Speak Truth to Power: A Quaker Search for an Alternative to Violence* (Philadelphia: American Friends Service Committee, 1955).
15. Martin Luther King, "The Montgomery Story," address delivered at the forty-seventh NAACP convention in San Francisco, June 27, 1965. (Circulated by SCLC.)
16. Martin Luther King, *Stride Toward Freedom: The Montgomery Story* (New York: Harper & Row, 1958), p. 219.
17. *Ibid.*, p. 217.
18. *Ibid.*, p. 224.
19. Bertrand Russell, "The Superior Virtue of the Oppressed," *Unpopular Essays* (New York: Simon and Schuster, 1950), pp. 58–64.
20. King, *Stride Toward Freedom*, *op. cit.*, p. 220.
21. James Peck, *Cracking the Color Line* (New York: CORE, ca. 1961).
22. Hayden, *op. cit.*, p. 14.
23. Robert McAfee Brown and Frank Randall, *The Freedom Riders: A Clergyman's View, an Historian's View* (New York: CORE, n.d.).

CHAPTER 4

Allies in the Wings

In the preceding chapter we discussed the roots of CORE's doctrine of nonviolence and the ideology as it developed during the period 1961–1963. This ideology, like the direct action movement, was in transition. Internal developments and external influences were bringing about changes in the outlook of the rank-and-file members and, ultimately, in CORE's official philosophy. This chapter examines the two ideological positions that made up CORE's nearest neighbors: one, greater militancy; the other, greater moderation. Both viewpoints had their strong adherents within CORE, and nearly every activist wrestled with the issues presented by these conflicting perspectives.

Black Nationalism

The "extreme militant" position was composed of two very different approaches: black nationalism and the far left in American politics—ranging from communist through Trotskyist to social democratic. A third position, that of Robert Williams, exiled former leader of the Monroe, North Carolina, NAACP, combined elements of the black nationalists and the far left and added the special ingredient of legitimizing the use of violent self-defense as part of direct action. All these approaches were radical in the sense that they involved basic theoretical rejections of the existing society, although the theories did not necessarily lead to immediate radical consequences in the realm of action.

The main tendency of black nationalism has been apolitical and "retreatist" vis-à-vis the white power structure.[1] The Muslims' doctrine of the white man's apocalyptic downfall really left the doing to Allah, thus freeing the members to follow the more pertinent doctrines involving middle class virtues and individual upward mobility. The preaching of extreme hatred for white America and the doctrine of the right of violent self-defense had an expressive or psychological, rather than an instrumental or directive, function. Since the members' activities were directed away from contact with the white power structure, the exhortations to hatred and self-defense really functioned only to build up their own businesses, to establish stable, middle class family lives, and to hold down regular jobs.

These same doctrines had a profound effect on direct actionists, for whom such ideas did have immediate behavioral consequences. The Muslims were very successful in laying bare the unconscious double standard that motivated the adherence of many whites and Negroes to nonviolence. They repeatedly pointed out that nonviolence was a special form of behavior required only of Negroes in a white culture that excelled in violence of all kinds and never abjured the use of violence in self-defense. The Muslims interpreted nonviolence not as the Negro's noble cross borne for a sinning culture, but as merely another version of the Negro's chains, clapped on this time by white liberals who controlled the integration movement and dampened its militancy with the aid of dupes like the Reverend King. Criticism of King's nonviolent doctrine was tied into the Muslims' attack on the whole Christian "slave religion," which had taught black people to accept oppression submissively since the beginning of slavery. "How long do you think we'd last," asks a Muslim speaker, "if the white man thought we'd all bow our heads and present our necks to the axe? About long enough for him to get the axe." [2]

The Muslims joined the far left in seeing the Negro problem as part of the larger problem of colonialism and in denouncing the United States as the leader of the new imperialist forces in the world. They identified enthusiastically with the free nations in Africa, with the Castro regime in Cuba, and with the socialist experiments in Egypt and other non-European areas. Capitalism also came under fire as a white system that choked out the small Negro businessman through a combination of racism and monopoly capitalism.[3]

The Muslims' greatest challenge to direct actionists was their insistence on speaking for the lower classes—the "masses" —of Negroes and their outstanding success in recruiting these elements in the Northern cities. CORE also saw itself as a mass movement concerned with the most disinherited of the race; but in most areas it was singularly incapable of mobilizing large numbers of lower class Negroes. During the early 1960s,

CORE leaders at the national and local levels began considerable soul searching into their failure to compete successfully for the allegiance of the Northern Negro masses. They became increasingly aware that the middle class makeup of most chapters had automatically led to a program that stressed the opening of white-collar jobs rather than factory jobs and the opening of middle class rather than lower class housing.[4]

On the ideological level, CORE chapters began to play down those aspects of their ideology that conflicted with Muslim philosophy and with many natural inclinations of the Northern ghetto population. Opposition to black chauvinism and emphasis on social integration were increasingly soft-pedaled, and nonviolence was played down in favor of an emphasis on militance in the struggle against the white power structure. In their debate with the Muslims, the direct actionists' best argument was that the Muslim approach really failed to confront white power, but led instead to a retreat into individual or, sometimes, to small collective attempts at upward mobility. The direct actionists' greatest weakness in the debate was precisely the practical and psychological threat that such a confrontation held for most lower class Negroes, to whom the Muslim ideology held out the sanctuary of retreat into an all-Negro world. This was the point at which CORE made its ideological stand against the Muslims.

In his book *Freedom When?* (1965), James Farmer argued that Negroes could not "change the manifest meaning of their separated existence solely by the force of their own wills." And, Farmer added, "If in his heart of hearts, the Negro believes that self-separation is only a rationalization for cowardly acceptance of segregation, then separation will fail." [5]

Although the formal CORE position during this period was against official cooperation with Muslims and other nationalist groups, in the North there was a great deal of debate and communication between members of both groups. The following excerpt from an informal conversation between CORE chief James Farmer and leaders of Bay Area CORE groups brings out the extent to which CORE leaders were struggling to come to terms with their nationalist competition:

F: I recognize that cooperation can be a trap, but we must recognize their [the nationalists'] emotional appeal.

FARMER: Tremendous!

F: We have to think how do we reach the masses.

J: CORE has failed because we are afraid to get down on the street with those masses of people who are really seeking something. The people most vulnerable are the people seeking for identification, and we don't reach them.

K: *All* Negroes have a foot in the door of nationalism and CORE must accept that—it's tied into the need of the black man to change his imagery. Nationalism is much broader than the Muslim movement. The Afro-Americans here have the power in the colleges. Besides, discrimination is a secondary problem compared to the need for a psychological solution to the problem: to dig being black—do you dig that? As Negroes become whole, lines of communication with whites have to be kept open—that's why I dig CORE.

FARMER: There isn't a quarrel or contradiction between the search for identity and CORE. Nationality groups dig being what they are—Negroes have lacked this—now he is developing pride . . . we can have this identity and still be for integration. The weakness of the Muslims is that they are not clear on the segregation-integration bit. It's a question of a program of Negro jobs through Negro business as against wiping out job discrimination. Should we all live together or be free to live where we choose? Malcolm X agrees with me that we should have a choice.

N: I don't believe the Muslims are really after separation, but they are representing an accurate dissent from American opinion. I think it's valid that the battle has to be fought on many fronts. CORE represents the middle class battle and isn't concerned with the lower class Negro—and maybe it needn't be. Middle class Negroes can't talk the language of the lower class—and is always rejecting them, even on a color basis.

G: Where we have CORE groups working on community problems, this whole problem falls into place—people find themselves able to cope with it. Here it seems to take over the whole arena. If you get into action, the enthusiasm carries people along.

W: I agree, but the significant thing is that CORE is the one group outside the nationalist arena where these things can be discussed and this is important. It is important that the conversation should carry on.

C: It seems to me the strong point of the Muslims is their newspaper—and the way they criticize things as they are . . . they rock the boat.

W: They have all the other groups looking at themselves.[6]

Just as CORE leaders found it necessary to moderate their line against racism and violence and to approach the nationalists gently, so the nationalists tended to soften their position vis-à-vis direct action groups. The Muslim newspaper, *Muhammad Speaks,* always carried sympathetic coverage of integration activities side by side with philosophical attacks on the idea of integration. Both nationalists and direct actionists found themselves in wry agreement on the truth and usefulness of Malcolm X's paradoxical statement that "when the Negroes see the hypocrisy of the white man in this integration struggle they won't want to integrate, but separate from him. And, on the other hand, when the whites realize that the Negroes would separate and follow the Honorable Elijah Muhammad—they will be more willing to integrate." [7]

The Far Left*

With the exception of the social democrats, the far left generally stressed the relationship between the domestic race problem and America's role as leader of the colonialist nations in their struggle against revolutionary movements in the underdeveloped, nonwhite areas of the globe. An author in *Freedomways* summed up the indictment by saying, "American racism has become an export commodity sold to every reactionary force in the world . . ." [8] Castro was praised for overcoming the racism that had been imported into Cuba by Americans:

> The Cuban experience has proved again what perceptive observers have known all along. Simply stated, it is that necessary social change need not wait on the patient education and persuasion of the bigot and the reactionary. Who can doubt that if a government as powerful and as rich as the U.S. were to throw its full legal and moral weight behind measures to eliminate racial discrimination it could achieve remarkable results overnight? . . .[9]

* This analysis uses a range of leftist sources from *The National Guardian,* a newspaper that strongly reflects the communist position; *The Militant,* a Trotskyist paper put out by the Socialist Labor party; *Freedomways,* a quarterly magazine devoted to the Negro protest movement and featuring writers from the whole range of leftist and black nationalist opinion; and Tom Kahn's *Unfinished Revolution* (1960), put out and circulated by the Social Democratic Federation. The many variations between these schools of thought will not be detailed here. Rather, the analysis dwells only on the broad features that they have in common and that are most relevant to the direct action movement.

The race problem was tied in with a complete rejection of the American economic system. The point was continually made that racism was not an isolated failure of the American system but merely the most dramatic symptom of its basic rottenness. In one of its editorials, *Freedomways* commented:

> Even as we chop away at one branch after another of political and social discrimination on the lynchers' tree of Negro oppression, the tap root that gives it its poisonous life is the economic exploitation of the Negro by those who occupy the top rungs of power in our contemporary exploitative society.[10]

The Militant likewise concluded that racial oppression was caused by "the drive for profit and politically the desire to keep the exploited divided and fighting each other along color lines so that they can't unite against their common exploiter." [11] More specifically, Tom Kahn reported the gains accruing to capitalism as a result of racial oppression:

> What does Big Business in America get out of this: According to the National Labor Service, "minorities . . . would have earned $72 billion (per year)." That's $30 billion a year in stolen wages! Is it any wonder that business interests in the Republican Party line up with the Dixiecrats to defeat meaningful civil rights legislation in Congress? . . .[12]

In its analysis of the problem, the left strongly emphasized economic factors in the race situation and concomitantly de-emphasized the psychological factors that were stressed by the nonviolent philosophy. The left saw the problem as one of economic and political power. It did not give way to notions of reform through amazing feats of nonviolent persuasion. Because of this emphasis on power and the fact that it tied the race problem in with a broader analysis and criticism of the society, the left tended to look beyond the direct action strategy to some broad alliance of forces that would permit a drive for power along conventional political lines. The fate of the Negro protest was bound up with the fate of unorganized labor, the labor movement, and the unemployed. The civil rights movement was seen as the only hope for these other groups, because it was the only vital and militant force in American politics, but it was dependent for its ultimate success on an alliance with other radical or potentially radical groups. Kahn recommended a third party combining labor, liberals, small farmers, and disadvantaged minorities. While admitting that the labor movement had been inactive on the problem of civil rights and generally conservative on all questions, Kahn saw underlying forces working to bring labor and the Negroes together:

> The labor movement *must* ally itself with the Negro, not out of any inherent morality or tolerance, but because of its very social nature. The non-unionized Negro is a potential scab. Moreover, the cheap labor which he and other minority groups are forced to provide tends to drag down the wages of other workers. Therefore, out of labor's own interest it must open its ranks to Negroes, strive for their inclusion and become their primary allies in the civil rights movement.[13]

The economic viewpoint leads quite naturally to pessimism about the possibility of solving the race problem through direct action. National labor secretary of the NAACP Herbert Hill, for example, noted that despite the gains made by direct action, the Negro was so hard hit by rising unemployment rates that his income and employment situation were actually deteriorating. He saw only two alternatives: an increasingly radical alliance between Negroes and unemployed white workers; or increasing degeneration and impotence until the civil rights movement could make status gains for middle class Negroes but bring about no real improvement in the economic position of the great mass of Negro workers.[14]

The left, which was predominantly white and advocated a broad coalition of Negroes and disadvantaged white groups on the basis of common economic interest, did not support the separatism and inverse racism of the black nationalists. It was, however, sympathetic to the radical mood of the black nationalists and frequently used this mood as a threat to beat the lagging white liberals into a more militant position. *The Militant* accused liberals of slowing down the pace of the civil rights movement by their claim that changes cannot be made "overnight":

> Overnight has been a long long time, not just years or decades but centuries. And what is "obvious" to the white liberal is no longer obvious to the Negro . . . Suppose they are wrong about this modern version of pie-in-the-sky-if-only-the-Negro-will-wait-and-do-as-he-is-told-in-the-meantime? It will be no skin off their backs. It isn't the Kennedys or Roses who are being advised to wait another *half of a lifetime* before they can hope to be treated as first-class citizens.[15]

A contributor to *Freedomways'* "reader's forum" said of the liberals:

I am convinced that their "sympathetic involvement" on the side of Negro rights has done as much to prevent the full attainment of those rights as the efforts of the thousands and thousands of bigots who have openly opposed equality of opportunity in the U.S.[16]

Along with the other "white liberals," the Kennedy administration came in for bitter criticism. The late playwright Lorraine Hansberry suggested:

Without waiting for another two men to die, that we want those troops to finish the Reconstruction in Alabama, Georgia, Mississippi, and every place else where the fact of our federal flag flying creates the false notion that what happened at the end of the Civil War was the defeat of the slaveocracy at the political as well as the military level . . .[17]

The economic interpretation of the Negro problem was slow to penetrate the thinking of rank-and-file CORE members, particularly in the South. There were, however, strong tendencies in this direction among the more alert and educated Negro and white members in the North. *Freedomways,* if not the white "left" press, was read by many Negro intellectuals in the Northern groups, and the leftist viewpoint was introduced by many white CORE members, products of this ideological tradition.

Legitimation of Self-Defense: Robert Williams

In the early 1960s, the solitary figure of Robert Williams served as a litmus test separating the Negro and white direct actionists from the rest of the prointegrationists in America. Significantly, it was a test in which the black nationalists, the left wing, and the direct actionists came out on the same side. To most liberal Americans, Williams' name was unfamiliar. If they had seen his picture hanging in their local post office along with other men wanted by the FBI for desperate crimes, they had probably accepted the FBI's description of him as a "wanted kidnapper, dangerous, probably armed." But to direct actionists—especially in the North, where access to dissident opinion was greater than in the South—Williams was not a criminal but a victim of segregationists, framed by North Carolina law enforcement officials and the FBI. He was a political figure who represented a controversial but important new position.

CORE's official position on the Williams case was a discreet silence. The NAACP suspended him from membership at the same convention at which it upheld, in theory, the right of self-defense. But Williams' future significance could not be judged by these responses any more than it could be judged by the overwhelming silence of the white press. He was the first Negro leader who tried to legitimize the use of violent self-defense in connection with direct action.

Williams took over leadership of the NAACP in Monroe, North Carolina, after the chapter had been almost completely destroyed by Klan intimidation. He rebuilt the organization with lower class Negro personnel and trained them to defend themselves against the incursions of the Klan. No publicity was given Williams' early and successful struggle to protect his membership against violence with violence. In 1959, however, the press carried a statement that made him a controversial figure in NAACP circles. After a Monroe court had freed a white man accused of attempted rape and assault on a Negro woman but had sentenced a Negro to two years in jail for catching the arm of a white woman during an argument, he made the following comment to reporters: "Since the Federal government will not bring a halt to lynching in the South, and since the so-called courts lynch our people legally, if it's necessary to stop lynching with lynching, then we must be willing to resort to that method." [18]

During the summer of 1961, Williams became involved in nonviolent direct action demonstrations organized in Monroe by former freedom riders. He agreed to let the demonstrators conduct their lines nonviolently, but he continued preparations to defend the Negro community with guns as the pressure of white reaction mounted. In the midst of this tense situation, Williams and several of the freedom riders were charged with kidnapping a white couple and holding them as hostages in exchange for the freedom of Negro demonstrators being held in the Monroe jail. The FBI backed the local charges and began a manhunt for Williams, who fled to Cuba.

Williams' version was that the white couple, Klan members, drove through the armed Negro community at the height of the racial tension and that he saved their lives by keeping them in his home until he could persuade the enraged Negroes to give them safe passage out of the area. The relative merits of Williams' and the FBI's versions of the incident cannot be decided here. What is important is that Williams' version was believed by most direct actionists. From Cuba, he began circulating a newsletter and broadcasting to the United States. He also published a book in this country, entitled *Negroes with Guns,* in which he developed his philosophy of violent self-defense.

Williams did not advocate violent reprisals against Southern whites. Neither did he accept passive resistance. What he did advocate was "flexibility in the freedom struggle." This meant nonviolent tactics where feasible and peaceful demonstrations where they were protected by law. But where there was a breakdown of law and order, he argued that the citizen had a right to protect his person, his family, his home, and his property. "To me," said Williams, "this is so simple and proper that it is self-evident." [19]

Like the Muslims, Williams considered nonviolence debasing to the Negro:

> As a tactic, we use and approve non-violent resistance. But we also believe that a man cannot have human dignity if he allows himself to be abused, to be kicked and beaten to the ground, to allow his wife and children to be attacked, refusing to defend them and himself on the basis that he's so pious, so self-righteous, that it would demean his personality if he fought back.[20]

Nonviolence, he felt, was based on a double standard that conveniently ignored the enormous violence being practiced daily in behalf of the status quo:

> When people say that they are opposed to Negroes "resorting to violence" what they really mean is that they are opposed to Negroes defending themselves and challenging the exclusive monopoly of violence practiced by white racists . . .[21]

Williams' analysis of the causes of racism and its cures took a leaf from the left as well as from the nonviolent philosophy. With the nonviolent theorists, who treated racism as primarily a problem of attitudes, Williams held that racism was a mental disease. But he turned it from a remediable ailment into a "mass psychosis" that would probably have to be cured, after the victory of the Negro movement, by "some sort of institution that will correct those Americans whose minds are thoroughly warped by racism . . .[22] With the left, he believed racism to be a fundamental part of the economic and social structure. And, even more than most left-wing writers, he emphasized that the privileged group in such a system could not be made to abdicate their position without force:

> The stranglehold of oppression cannot be loosened by a plea to the oppressor's conscience. Social change in something as fundamental as racist oppression involves violence. You cannot have progress here without violence and upheaval, because it's a struggle for survival for one and a struggle for liberation for the other. Always the powers in command are ruthless and unmerciful in defending their position and their privileges . . .[23]

This truth, he warned, would come out most clearly when Negroes stopped asking for things that whites didn't really care about—like integrated buses, on which most whites didn't ride anyway—and began to fight for the right to earn the same amount of money.[24]

Having assessed the ruling class as somewhat insane and completely ruthless in defense of their privileged position, Williams argued that they were also most unrelenting when they could practice violence with impunity. When Negroes were armed, and especially when disturbances might mean danger to white lives as well as Negro lives, then local authorities moved to keep order.[25]

Williams agreed with the far left in identifying racism with imperialism:

> Wherever there is oppression in the world today, it is the concern of the entire race. My cause is the same as the Asians against the imperialist. It is the same as the African against the white savage. It is the same as Cuba against the white supremacist imperialist . . .[26]

He agreed with the Muslims that white liberals backed the integration movement for the sole purpose of subverting it to a crippling commitment to nonviolence: "It is because our militancy is growing that they (the white liberals) spend hundreds of thousands of dollars to convert us into pacifists . . ."[27]

Williams' significance lay precisely in the fact that he took the Muslims' black nationalist and self-defense positions and the far left's overall condemnation of American economic and social structure and focused them on the area of direct action. These theories were relatively harmless within the confines of the Muslim or left-wing groups because the former withdrew from contact with the white power structure and the latter thought in terms of conventional political action. Williams merged their doctrines, however, to legitimate a significant revision of behavior: Race pride and pessimism about the ruling class provided the emotional fuel for a turn toward violent self-defense on the front lines of the direct action struggle.

Williams' thought presented a real issue to the more intellectual and vocal of the Northern CORE members, just as the practical exigencies of self-defense presented a pragmatic and immediate issue to Southern members. In informal conversations, CORE leaders predicted that violent self-defense was coming—indeed, was already a reality in many Deep South areas, where the Negro communities were arming and organizing for self-defense. While official CORE ideology continued to stress nonviolence, on the local level there was considerable cooperation with and sympathy for self-defense measures.[28] In the North, where self-defense was more a philosophical and psychological issue than an immediate practical one, the emphasis on nonviolence was continually toned down. Two field secretaries operating in the North, both of whom were at one time deeply committed to nonviolence, commented in 1962 that "in meeting with Northern CORE groups, we don't talk about nonviolence anymore." [29]

Probably the most immediate and pervasive effect of the militant ideological influences on CORE was to make the coercive aspects of nonviolent direct action more acceptable and legitimate. The ideological and practical possibility of violence extended the range of feasible positions radically and consequently shifted the "center" or "moderate" civil rights position. Open and energetic economic coercion of whites was no longer the most extreme possibility; beyond it loomed violent conflict. Thus, the stress on nonviolence as an instrument of conversion and persuasion was becoming less necessary as a legitimation for most adherents and allies of the movement.

Ideologies on the Conservative Boundary

White liberals were strongly attracted to the official version of nonviolence and tended to accept it at face value. They frequently took more interest in Gandhi's theory and example than did the direct actionists, they had great faith in its effectiveness, especially as a mover of hearts and an awakener of conscience. Probably no direct action leader could have scored Robert Williams in such absolute terms as Harry Golden did when he said:

> The NAACP expelled Williams because of his constant threat of violence, a threat which I believe would completely defeat the entire program and set us all back another ten years. The racists love Williams for this I can assure you, because they know in their hearts that the program of nonviolence and the constant writs before a judge will win this great sociological victory and eliminate the concept of a second-class citizenship in our country.[30]

Many white liberals differentiated between those direct action tactics that they felt were designed to arouse conscience and those that they condemned as mere pressure tactics. Thus, the Southern Regional Council in its report on the freedom rides praised the sit-in movement for "bringing the white South into agreement that old customs were unfair," but felt that the freedom ride was less effective because it was largely manned by outsiders and consequently engendered local opposition rather than understanding.[31] After quoting at length from SCLC literature on the philosophy of passive resistance, a *New York Times* article said:

> Where the demonstrators have been residents of the community involved, news reports have focused attention of whites on the problem and have caused some of them to question the morality of continued segregation and discrimination. This has not been nearly so true where the participants have been outsiders, as was the case in Birmingham.[32]

Although the writer recognized that gains had been won in Birmingham, he deplored the fact that they were won by "fear of disturbance" rather than by change of heart. Another writer said that although the freedom ride campaign was conducted in the spirit of Gandhian idealism

> it is also being waged with loud advance publicity and in deliberate defiance of state laws and local customs. There can be no question that in the "Freedom Riders" completely legal action there is an element of incitement and provocation in regions of high racial tension.[33]

The objection behind these statements was not to the presence of outsiders—really a spurious accusation in the case of Birmingham—but to the initiation of actions involving violence, for the liberals' attitude toward nonviolence was one of real concern for avoiding public disturbance, rather than a mere concern for legitimating a seemingly drastic tactic.

When direct action leaders warned the liberals that the Negro might turn to violence and nationalism, they were clearly more interested in mobilizing liberal support than in preventing these tendencies from developing. They were, indeed, well aware of the blackmail value of these tendencies and of the difficulty of moving the liberal public without such threats. The liberals, on the other hand, were sincerely afraid of these tendencies. They found it difficult to understand the temporizing of direct action leaders vis-à-vis radical groups, since they believed themselves to be allied with the integrationists against black nationalism and also violence. Direct actionists, however, generally saw themselves either as standing between the liberals and the Muslims or, if sides had to be chosen, as more allied with the Muslims and Robert Williams' school than with the white liberals. Both a racial and an ideological identity made this alliance appealing. Social scientist Daniel Bell expressed the liberals' criticism of this state of affairs when he said:

> It is an index of the fever pitch of the color issue that few Negro spokesmen are now willing openly to condemn the Black Muslims, although they were six months ago . . .
> Muslimism legitimizes violence and could be very dangerous . . . By lending respectability to such a movement the Negro intelligentsia is badly compromising itself.[34]

Underlying the liberals' devotion to persuasive rather than coercive tactics and to strict nonviolence and avoidance of disruptive situations was their assumption that discrimination was an isolated and shallow-rooted attitude that could be overcome with relatively mild methods. This assumption was shared by the official nonviolent philosophy, but there is no doubt that liberals believed it more deeply than persons involved in the direct action movement. The liberal view of American racism must be understood in the light of the average white liberal's background and outlook. Most liberals moved almost exclusively in liberal circles. They were usually unaware of the full extent of discrimination in their own communities and were genuinely shocked when it came to their notice. Judged from the isolated fastnesses of their liberal, often academic, environments, racism did indeed appear as an isolated and peculiar phenomenon. The reason that many moderate Negro leaders seemed to share this viewpoint is best explained by the fact that, being generally middle or upper class, these Negroes were isolated from the worst effects of racism. Also, being leaders of established groups like the NAACP, they were trapped within the confines of organizations better equipped to persuade than to coerce. Hence, it was decidedly in their interest to denigrate the need for coercion.

Liberals were generally convinced that the "liberal establishment," consisting of the administration, the Democratic party, labor unions, and the liberal churches were doing an excellent job on the integration front. The contrast between this position and the direct action position came out more clearly in their respective attitudes toward the administration. Joseph Kraft, the *Harper's* Washington correspondent, was typical in his praise. He credited Robert Kennedy with desegregating major transportation terminals by the use of government pressure. He also saw enormous progress on the voting front:

> By painstaking analysis of electoral rolls, the right to vote is being enforced in dozens of counties in the South. Already Negroes who never voted before have shifted the balance away from segregationists in some counties in Mississippi and Alabama . . . However slow the pace, however spotty the progress, the present justice department has done more than any agency of the government at any time, to help Negroes with the battle for equality.[35]

Whereas direct actionists judged the administration by its ability to enforce equal rights, liberals typically judged it by comparison with past achievement, the classical "conservative" perspective. The radical guideline of the direct actionists—not history or present reality, but "Freedom Now"—was alien to the liberals. Hence, they lamented that "one of the ironies of the struggle in the South is that these leaders [integrationists] direct much of their bitterness, not at their enemies the local segregationists, but at their friends in the Federal government." [36]

Liberals were also firm believers in the importance of the moderates, or middle ground. This belief was, in part, realistic, but it also stemmed from their faith in direct action as a persuasive technique that had to win over majorities in order to be effective. Thus, many liberal writers urged the movement to take care lest its overly militant tactics immobilize the forces of moderation and lose them the support of the middle ground. Direct actionists, by contrast, discounted the moderates almost completely because they believed that direct action succeeded by putting specific pressures on specific targets, rather than by winning over majorities. Also, the speed with which they wished to move toward their goal was so far removed from the concept of speed held by the moderates that it was difficult for the direct actionists, from their great ideological distance, to differentiate between the moderates, the conservatives, and the outright segregationists. The liberals, on the other hand, finding themselves midway between the direct actionists and the moderates, were continually threatening the one with the other in order to draw them closer together, to their own intermediate position.

Liberals tended to stress the realities of Negro underachievement and underqualification and to insist that some of these faults must be remedied before the integration movement could push for complete equality. Direct actionists tended either to deny these realities or to insist that they be dealt with through compensatory education and compensatory hiring. That is, to the extent that they admitted Negroes to be underqualified, they insisted that the burden lay on the white community and thus necessitated speedier rather than slower reform. Liberals found compensatory treatment hard to swallow. They continued to campaign for "color blindness" while direct actionists campaigned for preferential treatment.[37] This difference in outlook could also be put down to a difference in time perspective. The liberal envisioned a history of gradual progress with more to be attained in the future. Such progress, to be solidly founded, had to coordinate the various aspects of the race question: increasing Negro qualification had to be coordinated with further pushes toward integration. The direct actionist envisioned a history of injustice that was to be remedied immediately and by every instrument at hand.

The white liberal and Negro moderate positions represented the pull of the past within CORE. This was the ideological starting point for many who joined the movement and it resembled, in many ways, the attitudes of CORE itself before 1960. But with the freedom rides the very momentum of the movement led to increasing radicalism. The term "white liberal" became an epithet within CORE, and whites quickly learned to dissociate themselves from this position. Negro moderation of the NAACP style was generally associated with the hated characteristic of "Uncle Tomism." After 1964, internal and external developments combined to completely undermine the more conservative ideological influences around and within CORE. The various strands of nationalist and leftist militance were taken up and woven into a new kind of emerging CORE ideology.

NOTES

1. Unless otherwise specified, the general statements about Muslim ideology in this section are taken from the very excellent book by E. U. Essien-Udom, *Black Nationalism: A Search for Identity in America* (Chicago: University of Chicago Press, 1962).

2. Eric C. Lincoln, *The Black Muslims in America* (Boston: Beacon Press, 1961), p. 153.

3. "Negro Firms Battle to Survive Chain's Power," *Muhammad Speaks,* January 15, 1963.

4. See, for example, Marvin Rich, "Civil Rights Strategy After the March," *New Politics,* 11 (Fall, 1963), 43–52.

5. James Farmer, *Freedom When?* (New York: Random House, 1965), pp. 117–118.

6. Meeting between James Farmer and Bay Area CORE leaders and members, Berkeley, October, 1962.

7. From a television news program, August, 1962.

8. William L. Patterson, "The Negro Citizen and the Government," *Freedomways,* I (Summer, 1961), 193.

9. Julian Mayfield, "The Cuban Challenge," *Freedomways,* I (Summer, 1961), 188.

10. "The Economic Status of Negroes," *Freedomways,* II (Summer, 1962), 230.

11. Tom Kahn, *The Militant,* February 11, 1963, p. 6.

12. *Ibid.*

13. *Ibid.,* p. 36.

14. Herbert Hill, informal conversation, Berkeley, California, September, 1963.

15. Kahn, *op. cit.,* p. 6.

16. John A. Martin, Jr., "Reader's Forum," *Freedomways,* III (Winter, 1963), 94.

17. Lorraine Hansberry, "A Challenge to Artists," *Freedomways,* III (Winter, 1963), 35.

18. Julian Mayfield, "Challenge to Negro Leadership: The Case of Robert Williams," *Commentary,* 31 (April, 1961), 298.

19. Robert F. Williams, *Negroes with Guns* (New York: Marzani & Munsell, 1962), p. 40.
20. *Ibid.*, p. 121.
21. *Ibid.*, p. 114.
22. *Ibid.*, p. 111.
23. *Ibid.*, p. 110.
24. *Ibid.*, p. 116.
25. *Ibid.*, p. 40.
26. *Ibid.*, p. 72.
27. *Ibid.*, p. 113.
28. Informal conversation with CORE executive secretary James Farmer and CORE field director James McCain, fall, 1963.
29. Interview with Fredericka Kushner and Genevieve Hughes, both former West Coast field secretaries for CORE.
30. Harry Golden, quoted in an editorial in *The American Liberal* (November, 1962), p. 16.
31. Claude Sitton, "Regional Group Bids South Grant Freedom Ride Goals," *The New York Times*, May 31, 1961, pp. 1, 22.
32. Claude Sitton, "Passive Tactics Spread in Rights Battle," *The New York Times*, May 21, 1961, Sec. 11, p. 5.
33. "Alabama, U.S.A.," *The New York Times*, May 22, 1961, p. 30.
34. Daniel Bell, "The Tightrope of Color," *The New Leader*, July 8, 1963, pp. 8–9.
35. Joseph Kraft, "Riot Squad for the New Frontier," *Harper's*, August, 1963, pp. 73–74.
36. John Poppy, "The South's War Against Negro Votes," *Look*, May 21, 1963. For other articles taking a pro-administration line see: John Hope Franklin, "Emancipation Proclamation," *Crisis*, March, 1963; "Report on Washington," *Atlantic Monthly*, September, 1963; Eugene Rostow, "The Freedom Riders and the Future," *The Reporter*, June 22, 1961.
37. Murray Friedman, "The White Liberal's Retreat," *Atlantic Monthly*, January, 1963, pp. 42–46.

CHAPTER 5

Where They Came From

The active members of the Congress of Racial Equality were one of the "vanguard" groups of the direct action integration movement. They experimented with the new technique of direct action and introduced it to their communities all over the country; they led larger masses when these became involved from time to time; and they carried on the work of the movement between the surges of popular enthusiasm. They were among the first on the picket lines and in the jails, and they were also the deeply committed and involved people who steadily gave large amounts of time and energy to the day-to-day work of the direct action movement.

The activities of these CORE members were at variance with accepted American values in two ways. First, their commitment to full civil rights for the Negroes and to full integration of Negroes and whites was clearly deviant in a society that has always been overwhelmingly committed to Negro inferiority and separation of the races. Since CORE groups were in fact integrated organizations, membership in the group was much more real and visible a deviation than mere verbal or political commitment. As Lewis Killian says, "A liberal group which is biracial in composition may be regarded as even more dangerous and more distasteful than a militant Negro organization because it not only questions the validity of the norms but also violates them." [1]

Second, CORE members broke with traditionally accepted beliefs about proper tactics. In part, of course, their direct action tactics merely reflected a greater commitment to equality and integration, but direct action in and of itself constituted a radical break with accepted values. Civil disobedience and willingness to suffer arrest—indeed, that turn of mind that saw arrest and imprisonment as ennobling rather than degrading—were perhaps the strongest expressions of this aspect of direct action. Yet many less dramatic acts, such as appearing on the public sidewalk with a picket sign or engaging in open interracial cooperation and social intercourse, also reflected the peculiar and sharply deviant position into which interracial direct action plunged the participant. One had only to observe popular reaction to a picket line in any Southern or Northern city to grasp the extent to which such activities shocked most Americans. One had to have experienced what it meant for a Negro and a white to walk down a Southern city street together to grasp how outlandish such an act appeared to the average inhabitant.

Even the largest "mass movements" have activated only relatively small minorities, and these minorities have always been drawn from certain distinct and peculiar strata of their communities.[2] It should not surprise us, therefore, that CORE members did not represent a cross section of the white or Negro population. And, because the civil rights cause had a very different meaning for Negroes and whites in America, Negro and white CORE members did not always differ from the rank and file of their respective communities in exactly the same way. Integration was primarily a Negro cause supported by most Negroes. White members of CORE, on the other hand, were somewhat analogous to Marx's bourgeois intellectuals who abandoned their "true" class interest to make common cause with the working class.[3] Common sense would lead one to expect that white members would be much more unrepresentative of whites in general than is true of Negro members. Common sense also frequently raises the hypothesis of rebellion—especially the rebellion of the young against their parents—as an explanation of the motives that brought whites into the movement. In this chapter, the social characteristics of CORE members are examined in order to test these popular hypotheses and to develop some new generalizations about the social types who were recruited for nonviolent direct action.

The material in this chapter is based on information obtained from 148 officers and active members of local groups, plus a few paid staff members of the CORE national office. Information on 102 of these persons was collected by means of written questionnaires at two national CORE conventions, plus information from 46 respondents interviewed during the visits to local Southern and Northern groups.

Background of White Direct Actionists

The most striking single fact about the CORE whites is their high education level. Table 1 compares our sample with the white population of the United States.

TABLE 1 **Years of Education of Sixty White CORE Members and White Population of the United States**

	CORE	United States*
12 years or less completed	8%	82.6%
13–15 years completed	8	9.3
16 or more years completed	57	8.1
11–15 years, continuing†	27	—

* Based on the 1960 census.

† Because more than a quarter of our sample are students and the census figures are for persons twenty-five years of age or over, we have tried to make the categories more comparable by separating those between eleven and fifteen years who are continuing their education at the present time. Most of these persons will eventually be added to the category "16 or more years of education." Only one person in the sample was in high school.

As the figures in Table 1 suggest, the white respondents were drawn almost entirely from the highest occupational levels: 38 percent were in professional jobs and 18 percent in semiprofessional, proprietory, managerial, clerical, and sales jobs. The 25 percent who were students were generally headed for these two occupational levels; only 7 percent were drawn from blue-collar ranks. In addition, there were 8 percent housewives, 2 percent unemployed, and 2 percent full-time CORE staff members. Clearly, however, the militant CORE position was atypical of these high socioeconomic strata. The picture must be reviewed in more detail to get at the social characteristics leading to CORE membership.

Ten of the twenty-three professional persons who filled out the questionnaire were in the academic profession: four professors, three instructors, and three persons in academic research. The academic community was heavily represented, with fifteen students and ten academicians out of a total of sixty persons. Further, primarily the social science and humanities departments of major academic institutions supplied this element. In addition, there was a larger number of professionals who had undergone several years of postgraduate training in such departments.

The political groups in which the sample reported membership showed a very heavy representation in the range of opinion from liberal Democratic to social democratic left. Some 25 percent reported membership in one or more peace groups, including SANE, the Student Peace Union, the Committee for Nonviolent Action, Turn Toward Peace, War Resistor's League, and the U.S. Committee for the United Nations; 10 percent reported membership in the Socialist party or its youth branch, the Young People's Socialist League; and 23 percent reported a variety of liberal groups, most frequently the American Civil Liberties Union, Americans for Democratic Action, and the Liberal party of New York.*

According to Will Herberg, when Americans are asked to state their religious preference, 95 percent identify themselves as being Protestant, Catholic, or Jewish. Only 5 percent declare that they have no religious affiliation or preference.[4] Indeed, Herberg points out that "there is a tendency to regard all people who are not committed to one of the three great faiths as being disloyal to American principles and traditions." [5] Yet 53 percent of the white CORE members indicated that they had no religious preference. Whereas Herberg reports that 73 percent of his national sample considered themselves active members of a church,[6] only 12 percent of our CORE whites reported weekly church attendance and only 28 percent reported any church attendance whatever.

As is shown in Table 2, the whites who did list a religious

TABLE 2   Religious Preference of Twenty-seven Religious CORE Whites and United States Population*

	CORE Whites	United States†
Protestants	56%	71%
Catholics	11	25
Jews	26	4
Ethical Culture‡	7	—

* Figures are corrected to make them comparable; in both columns the percentages are based on those declaring a religious preference.

† See Will Herberg, *Protestant, Catholic, Jew* (Garden City, N.Y.: Anchor Books, 1960), p. 47.

‡ The Ethical Culture Society is a liberal agnostic-humanist group that functions as a religious denomination. It is too small to show up in national statistics, but it figures in our CORE data.

preference were drawn disproportionately from among the three major religious groups. Protestants were mildly underrepresented relative to their percentage in the population; Jews were strongly overrepresented, and Catholics were strongly underrepresented. In their study of ethnic groups in New York City, Nathan Glazer and Daniel P. Moynihan noted a similar tendency toward coalition of Jewish and Prot-

* Only one respondent listed membership in a Trotskyist or communist group. However, this figure may be an underestimation because the national CORE constitution prohibits membership to persons who belong to groups that expound a philosophy inimical to the fundamental principles of CORE, a clause that is interpreted as barring communists.

estant elements with Negro and Puerto Rican minorities against the predominantly Catholic ethnic groups.[7]

The degree of Jewish overrepresentation becomes even more marked if one looks at the entire white CORE sample and adds in those nonreligious persons who indicate their parents' religion as Jewish. The proportion of persons of Jewish descent in the entire sample now reaches one-third. But this is still a conservative estimate, for another 25 percent reported both themselves and their parents as having no religious affiliation. Undoubtedly some part of this group was also Jewish. Although most of these "ethnic Jews" were not religious, they still reflected and identified with many aspects of their Jewish background.

Looking at the characteristics of the white CORE sample —high education, high occupational status, academic connection, membership in liberal and left-wing groups, absence of religious affiliations, and overrepresentation of Jews and underrepresentation of Catholics—it is clear that these variables overlap. They point quite unmistakably to a definite subculture, that narrow layer of the intelligentsia that appears in the liberal to left-wing range of the political spectrum and in the social science and humanities departments of major academic institutions. On its radical, or "nonrespectable," border, this subculture merges into bohemia and the extreme left, communist, anarchist, and such. On its "respectable" boundary, it merges into the "establishment liberals," the moderately liberal pillars of universities, of the Democratic party, of liberal religious denominations, and of other established liberal institutions. This is a milieu that generally supports the integrationist zeal and the direct action activities of our respondents. If the social background of the approximately 65,000 financial supporters of CORE were analyzed, one would undoubtedly find that most of them were part of this same subculture, though unwilling or unable to go the length of personal involvement. It is clear, then, that although the CORE whites deviated from white opinion in general, most of them were in tune with the stratum that made up their social environment and their reference groups. Direct actionists constituted the radical wing of that environment, and their experiences and convictions in turn rebounded upon the environment to draw it toward a position of more militant support for the direct action movement.

It is often supposed that white members joined CORE as

an act of rebellion against their conservative or racist parents. But the data gathered belie this assumption. As Table 3 indicates, most of our white respondents come from families of the same high occupational status as themselves. Ten of the sixteen professional fathers were in occupations frequently associated with the liberal-left subculture: professors, scientists, artists, and writers.

TABLE 3 Occupations of Fathers (or Guardians) of Sixty White CORE Members

Professional	27%
Proprietor, manager, official	35
Clerical, sales	15
Skilled worker	12
Semiskilled, unskilled, custodial	3
Farmer	5
No answer	3

Parents' religion may provide a further clue to the parents' political attitudes. Jews, even when they are in such predominantly conservative occupations as business proprietorship, generally have more liberal views than their gentile counterparts. For the son of a Jewish proprietor to become a left-wing professional does not usually represent a sharp break with family values, and the transition will usually be shared by members of the respondent's peer group. Two other religious affiliations indicate an outlook similar to that of the CORE member offspring: first, the Unitarian and Universalist churches (see Table 4); and second, the category "no religious affiliation." *

The questionnaire data provide some indication that a little over half of the respondents had parents with views congenial to the values of the liberal-left subculture. The more detailed information available for the eighteen white CORE members in our sample provides stronger evidence in the same direction. Six of the eighteen interviewed reported that their parents were extremely liberal on racial matters. They re-

* The association between liberalism and "no religion" would not hold true if the parents were lower class. There, lack of religious affiliation is often a symptom of isolation from the community, lack of education, and so forth. Since most of our subjects are middle class and above, we may assume that no religious affiliation is symptomatic of a nonconformist attitude toward prevailing values. In many cases it probably also reflects Jewish ethnicity.

TABLE 4   **Religious Affiliation of 120 Mothers and Fathers of White CORE Members***

Protestant	33%
Catholic	14
Jewish	24
No religion	25
Unitarian, Universalist, Ethical Culture	5

* Because there were nine cases of parents with mixed affiliations, mothers and fathers were counted separately.

lated variously that their parents had Negro friends in the home, refused to live in segregated neighborhoods on principle, felt racial equality to be a religiously ordained principle, and talked a good deal about civil rights issues in the home. One respondent even reported that his mother joined CORE herself while he was away on the 1961 freedom ride. Five others described their parents as mildly liberal. In these homes the race problem was seldom discussed, but when it came up, the Negro was always spoken of with sympathy and the children were admonished that prejudice and name-calling were wrong. Some remembered seeing their parents behave in a strongly unprejudiced manner, even though the subject was not discussed—as in the case of one person who saw his father hire two secretaries from a minority group despite strong opposition from his other employees. In some cases the parents were mildly opposed to the more dangerous civil rights activities of the respondents, but only because they feared injury to their child.

Five respondents reported that their parents were somewhat prejudiced. Typical of these cases is the family of one Southern-born CORE member whose parents believed that Negroes were inferior but also stressed that he should always deal fairly with them. He recalls:

> I do remember where I would refer to a Negro woman as a lady when I was little and created quite a bit of amusement on the part of my parents . . . but they brought me up in an orthodox Baptist way, and really taught me to be nice to everybody so this just came natural to me. I was imbued with some of the better parts of the Southern tradition as well as the worst parts.

The same respondent said that although his parents could not approve of his jail-going activities from an ideological viewpoint, "they sympathize with me as their son." Only two respondents reported that their parents were markedly prejudiced and that they experienced conflict with them over the race issue.

Southern-born whites were very rare in CORE. Birthplace data were available on eight of the eleven white members in our sample who were currently active in Southern chapters. Of these, only three were born in Southern or Border states. The white participants in the South came from the same background as those in the North. Although the South offered less social support, the majority of these members were connected with academic institutions that provided at least some semblance of a sympathetic or neutral milieu.

In summation, it seems that rebellion against parents or current reference groups was a rare condition of adherence to a militant, direct action civil rights group. This is not to say that some respondents did not appear to be rebellious or to feel hostility toward parents and current associates; it is only to suggest that such rebelliousness is more often expressed within the political milieu in which people originate and live, rather than by deviation toward an opposite position. The contrary impression probably arises from the fact that the exceptional, dramatic case of rebellion and conversion stands out more sharply in the mind of the undisciplined observer than the far more frequent, nondramatic cases of those direct actionists who came out of families and subcultures that supported their views and actions.

Background of Negro CORE Members*

As Table 5 shows, Negro CORE members, like their white counterparts, were drawn from among the best-educated persons in their communities. Although the educational level of Negro members was somewhat lower than that of white members, the Negroes contrasted even more sharply with the general population from which they were drawn.

The data for Negro CORE members also indicate high-

---

* In 1963, Howard Zinn checked into the social background of forty-one SNCC field workers in Mississippi. His findings are very similar to my statistics on CORE. Of the thirty-five Negroes in the SNCC group, twenty-one had parents in unskilled or skilled working class jobs or in farming. Of the six whites, two were Southern-born and all were of middle class parents. Two-thirds of the entire group had some college education. Three-fourths were under twenty-two years of age. Howard Zinn, *SNCC: The New Abolitionists* (Boston: Beacon Press, 1964), pp. 9–10.

TABLE 5 **Years of Education of CORE Sample and United States Population by Race**

| | NONWHITE | | WHITE | |
	CORE	U.S.*	CORE	U.S.*
12 years or less	18%	92.1%	8%	82.6%
13–15 years	21	4.4	8	9.3
16 or more years	36	3.5	57	8.1
11–15 years, continuing in school	24	—	27	—
No answer	1	—	—	—

* Based on the 1960 census.

strata occupation distribution. Some 20 percent were in professional jobs and 25 percent in semiprofessional, proprietory, managerial, and sales jobs. Another 25 percent were students who were planning to reach these occupational levels. Only 10 percent were blue-collar workers.*

One must next consider how the respondents differ from others in the middle and upper middle class strata of Negro society. In the preceding section, it was shown that white CORE members came from a distinct subculture having values quite different from the bulk of the white middle and upper middle class. Because civil rights is, after all, a "Negro cause" and sympathy for it is prevalent throughout the Negro community, one would not expect to find such a marked difference between Negro CORE members and the rest of the Negro middle class. Moreover, although there is much anti-white feeling among Negroes, social integration meets with much less hostility than is true among whites. Thus, a Negro who took part in civil rights activities, even of the most militant sort, and who developed political and social bonds across the color line did not deviate as sharply from the prevailing values of his community as did the white member in a similar situation. This hypothesis was generally borne out; Negro CORE members were more like the community and class status out of which they came than were white CORE members.

No concentration in the academic professions was found among the Negro professionals in the sample. There was

* There were also 6 percent housewives, 2 percent unemployed, 8 percent CORE staff, and 4 percent for whom no occupational data were available.

only one professor. The seven teachers, three social workers, and three ministers in the group reflected the typical concentration of Negroes in these occupations. The remainder of the professionals were scattered over various fields. An examination of the college majors and occupational aspirations of the interview respondents also reflected a wider range of interests and plans than those found among our white respondents.

Organizational memberships provided more direct evidence on the political, civic, and social ties that helped make up the milieu of the Negro members. Membership in liberal-left political groups was relatively rare. Only ten persons, seven Northerners and three Southerners, listed such memberships. On the other hand, Negroes, much more frequently than whites, held membership in what may be termed "conventional civic" groups, such as the PTA, YMCA, and Scouts, and "moderate integrationist" groups, such as the NAACP and Urban League. Both kinds of groups are typical of the middle and upper class Negro community.

When asked to state their religious preference, 11 percent of the Negro CORE members put "no religion." Although this figure is over twice as high as the racially mixed proportion with no religious preference in Herberg's national sample, it falls dramatically short of the 55 percent reported by the white members. Only 21 percent of Negroes indicated no church attendance, as compared with 72 percent of the whites.

The overwhelming majority of the Negro respondents came from Methodist or Baptist homes. A scattering of other faiths was represented among the respondents' parents, and only one respondent reported parents with no religious affiliation. Three-fourths of the respondents remained with the religion of their parents. It is informative to examine the twenty-two persons who broke with their parents to see whether or not they seem to have moved sharply away from the standards of the Negro middle class community. Two types of changes occurred: (1) those symptomatic of upward social mobility but not necessarily representing a break with the middle class Negro community and its values, changes from Baptist or Methodist to Catholic, Episcopalian, Presbyterian, Congregational, or Lutheran; and (2) those indicating a definite break with traditional values, changes from any religious affiliation to no religion or to Ethical Culture (a predominantly white, agnostic-humanist group). Among the twenty-two "changers" there were twelve cases of upward mobility change and ten cases of change that broke with traditional values.

Having found that CORE Negroes generally resembled the Negro middle class community, one must raise the question of how they differed from middle class Negroes who did not join the direct action movement. And here one must raise a further and related question: What accounted for the pronounced hostility between CORE and the established middle class Negro leadership and community? *

In establishing the similarity of Negro members to the middle class community, the presence of a small number of deviants was also noted. There were sixteen persons who appeared to resemble the liberal-left subculture of most white members on the basis of one or both of the following characteristics: (1) having no religious affiliation and (2) listing membership in liberal-to-left political organizations. Closer scrutiny of these deviants reveals two other associated characteristics: Thirteen of the sixteen were from Northern chapters, and eleven of the sixteen (69 percent, compared with 26 percent for the remainder of the Negro sample) had fathers in professional and white-collar occupations. Only one had a father below the rank of skilled worker. Here was a small group of persons who came from solidly middle or upper class Negro homes[8] and who, perhaps in the course of attending universities and moving into professional jobs, were drawn into the liberal-left subculture. They may also be persons who were drawn into this subculture after joining CORE, as a result of their close association with liberal-left whites. The move into this subculture was one that could be made easily only by persons from high-status, well-educated families, since only such a background prepared Negroes to move comfortably within the intellectual and status level typical of this milieu.

Most of the seventy-two Negroes who made up the bulk of the sample were highly mobile. Typically, they were children of semiskilled or unskilled working class fathers who had risen to professional or clerical jobs. About half this group were under twenty-five years old and many were students. Thus, although they were bound for middle class occupations or had recently engaged in such occupations, they were still closely tied to their previous origins and certainly not yet

* This hostility will be discussed in some detail in Chapter 6.

firmly established in and committed to the middle class Negro community, with its strongly inhibiting codes of middle class respectability. The interview data also suggest that because the Negro CORE members had not yet shed their working class origins and because they tended to be darker skinned than members of the established older-generation middle class, they were not fully "socially acceptable" within the Negro bourgeoisie. One leader of a Southern CORE chapter revealed this tension in her comments about the established middle class Negro leadership with which she frequently had political dealings:

> We have this peculiar situation where some people think that they're Creoles, the light skinned ones from the old families, and they don't think they're Negroes. For instance, my mother works as a waitress at the D—— which is the real bourgeois Negro restaurant here, and I know that T—— [NAACP leader] thinks "what am I doing negotiating with them when my mother is a waitress at this place that he goes to?" And I guess if I weren't in college I'd really be at their mercy. That's the one reason they tolerate me . . . These people love to be important and the thing that makes me so mad about them is that they're supposed to be on our side. But they accept white values. The closer they get to looking white, the more they accept the white values.

In summary, there were two typical ways in which CORE members differed from the middle class Negro community. A small number appeared to be what might be called "post-bourgeois," in that they came, typically, from middle class parents but had moved beyond these origins into the liberal-left and predominantly white intelligentsia. A larger contingent could be termed "prebourgeois," in that they were in transition from the working class into the middle class, though not yet firmly established in the Negro middle class community.

The kind of radicalism associated with direct action for civil rights appears to stem not from great deprivation but from upward mobility. Indeed, militant political action may be seen as an extension of the mobility drive. The Negro student has made a successful jump out of the working class, but he sees further progress hampered by race barriers. He is getting a good education but sees himself blocked from a good job; or perhaps he has a good job but is barred from spending his money in a good restaurant or on a good apartment in a middle class neighborhood. Under such circumstances, that same energy and ambition could be shifted from the arena of individual mobility to that of collective political effort.

Upwardly mobile persons in the generation now in its forties and fifties also met these barriers, but the extremely repressive conditions of that time forced them to accommodate themselves to the limitations imposed by the white world. The CORE generation, growing up in a less repressive era, took a radically new and different course. In addition, as has been seen, the militancy of the "prebourgeois" Negro was spurred on by social barriers within the Negro community itself, barriers that closely reflected "white" values, such as the superiority of light skin and the prestige of a "respectability" modeled on the white middle class.

Availability for Direct Action

The two preceding sections showed that CORE members were recruited from relatively narrow strata within the white and Negro communities. The problem of recruitment may be pinpointed further by asking who, among the ideologically militant, actually joined a group like CORE.

Active membership in CORE made many demands for which only certain individuals were available. An unusually large amount of time and energy was required of active members. CORE may be characterized as a total involvement* organization in the sense outlined by sociologist Philip Selznick for the Communist party.[9] An active member or officer would usually attend two evening meetings every week and spend two more evenings telephoning, cutting stencils, passing out leaflets, and the like. During direct action campaigns he might spend almost every weekday evening and all day Saturday on picket lines. Usually, he would find CORE business "on his mind" all day—remembering to make a few phone calls from work, picking up paper for leaflets during his lunch hour, buttonholing fellow students between classes, and the like. Once or twice a year an active member would probably travel considerable distance to attend regional conferences, annual

---

* Since Selznick's use of the term "total involvement" also implies mechanisms for total ideological control from above, it can only be applied to CORE with reservations. CORE's structure is highly decentralized and democratic. It does serve to indicate, however, a similarity in the quality of the member's commitment, one that differentiates both organizations quite sharply from the usual political voluntary organization.

conventions, or direct action projects at the state or national capital. Chairmen of local chapters frequently dropped out of school or quit jobs during their tenure in order to devote the required time to the duties of their office. Turnover in most groups was very high. One of the most frequent reasons for resignation was the need to catch up on student or professional commitments that had been sacrificed; another frequent reason was the need to appease family complaints about the member's continual absence from home.

Members of direct action groups also had to be prepared to face the various formal and informal sanctions incurred as a result of their activities. In the South, these included loss of job, expulsion from school, arrest and confinement, and occasional violence and threats of violence against the participant and his family. Loss of respectability and its various consequences were also inevitable: the honor student in college was suddenly condemned by professors as a "troublemaker," and the professional found some of his valuable acquaintances and contacts turning against him. In the North the consequences were much less severe. The problem of social ostracism, especially severe for Southern whites, was not a major problem for Northern whites, for they generally moved in a milieu that accepted or even applauded their efforts. But arrest and lengthy jail sentences were increasingly coming to be the fate of Northern direct actionists. This was especially so as the movement turned more and more to civil disobedience tactics in order to influence businesses that were not as easily hit by boycotts and picket lines as were the earliest targets, such as retail outlets in Negro neighborhoods. Given these special requirements, more stringent in the South than in the North, what types of persons were "available" for direct action?

The extreme youth of the group was one of the most striking features of the CORE sample. Some 60 percent were under thirty years of age and 42 percent were under twenty-five. Only 14 percent were over forty. These figures are especially remarkable when one remembers that the sample is heavily weighted in the direction of officers and staff members. Southern chapter members were even more youthful than Northern members: 57 percent of the Southern members and 32 percent of the Northern members were under twenty-five.

Of course the age factor reflects more than availability. It has been frequently noted that the direct action movement is a generational phenomenon. Among Negroes, it seemed to be predominantly the younger generation—reared in an atmosphere of less fear and greater expectation than their elders —that had the optimism and courage to engage the status quo in open battle. Among whites there was also a generational factor in that the young grew up in an atmosphere of much greater racial liberalism, at least on a verbal level, than the generation of their parents or even their older brothers and sisters. In this sense, the age composition of CORE might be discussed in connection with the question of ideological militancy. Age is also a major factor influencing availability for direct action.

The very young were usually college students: 22 percent of the Northern members and 30 percent of the Southern members. Being a student is one of the safest positions from which to defy society. Most academic institutions, even in the South, provide a good deal of insulation and protection for their students. Also, this is a time when family commitments, career commitments, and community involvements are at a minimum.

Among those in the Southern groups who were not students, job safety was one of the main factors that made Negroes or whites available for direct action. The questionnaire data are not sufficiently detailed about the respondents' jobs to give us precise statistics, but it is evident that most Southern Negro members were in positions not easily controlled by white businessmen or politicians. They were ministers, professionals who catered to a Negro clientele, or proprietors, managers, or employees of Negro firms. It is striking to note, for instance, that whereas seven Northern Negroes were teachers, none of the Southern Negroes were, for teaching jobs in the South are extremely vulnerable to white political control. The older whites in Southern CORE groups were generally liberal clergymen who were protected by the nature of their congregation, academicians, and employees of the federal government or of large Northern-based firms.

Freedom from family obligations also made people available for direct action. Some 59 percent of our CORE members were single.* The number of children was not asked in

* Marital status was not asked in the first convention questionnaire. This percentage is based on the ninety-two cases from the second convention questionnaire and from the interviews.

the questionnaires, but was asked in the forty-six extended interviews. In this group we found that those persons who were most available, in the sense of having neither spouse nor children, constituted 46 percent; those of intermediate availability, that is, persons having either spouse or children but not both, constituted 22 percent; and those with low availability, people having both spouse and children, constituted 33 percent. Those figures are not merely reflections of the youthfulness of the group, for three-fourths of the interviewees were over twenty-one. Widowed and divorced persons and married people without children made up a large percentage of those in the higher age groups.

The absence of family ties was important in making people available for larger time commitments and for the absorption of social sanctions that would have had a more disruptive effect on people with families; it also reflected the nature of the local CORE chapter as a tightly knit, primary group. Extensive dedication to the group's activities always went along with the formation of absorbing primary group ties with other members. This type of involvement was both difficult for and psychologically unnecessary to people with extensive family commitments. Without this type of personal involvement, members seldom remained long or became very active in a group. The deep involvement and primary relations in CORE were among the major psychological rewards that the movement offered its members in return for the very considerable sacrifices it required.

Conclusions

The members of CORE generally had exceptionally high occupational and educational status. Yet they were not part of the established middle and upper middle class leadership of their respective racial communities. Most of the whites were drawn from the liberal-left political subculture typical of social science and humanities departments of large academic institutions as well as from certain artistic and social-problem centered professions. A minority of the Northern Negro members stemmed from middle class homes but had moved into the liberal-left milieu of the whites. The majority of Northern Negro members and almost all Southern Negro members were young people rising from working class origins into middle class professions but because of their background, youth, and racial characteristics were not yet established in Negro middle or upper class society. Finally, the Negroes and whites who became active in CORE were those most available for the high demands of direct action by virtue of their youth and lack of commitments to family or career.

This social composition made for certain distinct strengths and weaknesses in an organization dedicated to nonviolent direct action. One clear strength was the militancy of the membership. The relatively high status and upward mobility of the Negro members and the liberal-left subculture of the white members assured a certain basic willingness to make radical demands and to use unconventional tactics. In addition, the relative isolation of both groups from the established leadership and norms of the middle class freed them from the inhibitions that such ties would inevitably have exercised over the group's tactics.

Another strength lay in the fact that high educational and professional skills were requisite to the type of operation involved in CORE. Legal issues had to be understood, negotiators had to deal with businessmen, and resolutions had to be presented to city councils. This need for political sophistication was greater in the North than in the South. In the North, CORE groups carried on involved negotiations with large firms and government agencies, whereas in the South, more energy went into sit-ins and the serving of jail sentences. This difference was reflected in the lower educational levels, younger age, and lesser political experience of the Southern chapter members.

The high educational and occupational level of the CORE membership was also closely tied to nonviolence in the movement. Although one might speculate on the extent to which the absence of religious basis for nonviolence in this group was counteracted by the prevalence of pacifist influences, undoubtedly the strongest guarantee of nonviolent discipline was simply the aversion to physical violence that characterizes the life style of the middle class.

NOTES

1. Lewis Killian and Charles Grigg, *Racial Crisis in America: Leadership in Conflict* (Englewood Cliffs, N.J.: Prentice-Hall, 1946), p. 98.

2. Among many studies of this phenomenon, see Harold D. Lasswell, Daniel Lerner, and E. E. Rothwell, *The Comparative Study of Elites* (Stanford, Calif.: Stanford University Press, 1952); and William Kornhauser, *The Politics of Mass Society* (New York: Free Press, 1959), pp. 56–57, 179–193.

3. Karl Marx and Friedrich Engels, "Manifesto of the Communist Party," *Selected Works* (Moscow: Foreign Languages Publishing House, 1962), I, 43. Discussions of this phenomenon are found in Robert Michels, *Political Parties* (New York: Free Press, 1949), pp. 316–329; and Crane Brinton, *Anatomy of Revolution* (Englewood Cliffs, N.J.: Prentice-Hall, 1952), pp. 42–53.

4. Will Herberg, *Protestant, Catholic, Jew* (Garden City, N.Y.: Anchor Books, 1960), p. 46.

5. *Ibid.*, pp. 257–258.

6. *Ibid.*, p. 47.

7. Nathan Glazer and Daniel Patrick Moynihan, *Beyond the Melting Pot* (Cambridge, Mass.: MIT Press and Harvard University Press, 1963), p. 302.

8. Class levels for the Negro community are based on indications given by Frazier in his discussion of the Negro class system. Franklin Frazier, *Black Bourgeoisie* (New York: Free Press, 1957), pp. 23–24.

9. Philip Selznick, *The Organizational Weapon: A Study of Bolshevik Strategy and Tactics* (New York: McGraw-Hill, 1952), pp. 27–29.

CHAPTER 6

Case Study of a
Southern CORE Group

"I've been waiting two years for this. We've been working for it for two years, and I want to stay here until we find out what happened tonight." This was the thought shared by the nineteen members of the CORE chapter of "Southern City," gathered in a Negro Baptist church for their weekly meeting on a humid July evening in 1962; victory in their lunch-counter desegregation campaign seemed, incredibly, only hours away.

Everyone was acutely conscious that a Negro negotiating team was sitting across town with representatives of the white business community to set the date for simultaneous desegregation of all lunch counters in the city. CORE's two representatives were to report back to the CORE meeting as soon as the negotiations were completed. Then the chapter, restless under a suspension of direct action during the negotiating period, could begin organizing testing teams to ensure compliance.

For the past two years, Southern City CORE had weathered police harassment, arrest, violence, ridicule, and hostility as they picketed and sat-in at lunch counters in the downtown area. Even the established Negro leadership had frequently discouraged their effort and shown hostility to it. But the campaign had succeeded. There was no doubt about CORE's accomplishment. This small determined band had brought the white business community to the negotiating table and had made it willing to talk to "anybody who can stop these demonstrations."

But more was at stake than the lunch-counter victory. The unity of the Negro community was also on trial. For CORE, despite its often rancorous disagreements with older leaders of the Negro community, had voluntarily invited the Negro "establishment" into the negotiating committee. They felt that this was necessary to Negro unity although they continued to regard their Negro allies with suspicion.

Of the nineteen people gathered for the meeting, fifteen were Negroes and four were whites. All but three of the Negroes were college students or persons of student age. The vice-chairman opened the meeting with a matter-of-fact announcement that several persons whom the group had sent to participate in a national CORE project in North Carolina had been arrested. A girl sitting next to me whispered with obvious pride, "One of them is my sister."

Significantly, the discussion concerned not the white but the black community: "the Negro's attitude toward Africa." A dark girl in the front row started the discussion with a theme that would be repeated consistently. She referred only briefly to Africa and then went on to discuss the divisions and resentments in the Negro community: "Through observation all my life I have always seen the way Negroes joke about Africa, and also the attitude people have toward light and dark skins. People tease about black." She added that she hoped the test teams that would try the lunch counters after desegregation would include some really dark-skinned testers because "sometimes they might serve a light Negro but still turn a darker one away."

After dwelling briefly on the glories of ancient African empires, the discussion returned to the here and now. "I think we have a view of Africa from Tarzan movies." "Most Negroes only know the white man's culture." "Negroes are ashamed of Africa because we don't really know anything about it. We've let whites set our values." "Until black nationalism began to take hold—in the late 1950s—you could look at every outstanding Negro and see that he had a light-skinned wife. No matter if he was black as pitch himself."

According to the Negro community's system of color ranking, CORE members fell on the disfavored side. Color ranking was especially prominent in Southern City, where the light-skinned upper class had a long history of acceptance. In this connection, the Negro community rated people according to three interrelated criteria: hair quality, skin color, and membership in old families. Only two CORE members, one of them in the active nucleus of the group, ranked as "prestigeful" on the criteria of hair and skin color. None were connected with "old families."

After an hour and a half the meeting adjourned. The four whites and two Negroes left, and the rest wandered out to patronize the cold-drink machine. Gradually those remaining reassembled to await the arrival of the CORE negotiators. A round of singing began under the informal direction of one member. Some were familiar songs in the movement—adaptations from such spirituals as "Michael Row the Boat Ashore" and new versions of such labor protest songs as "Which Side Are You On?" The most interesting songs were very recent adaptations of popular songs. The previous summer's "Hip-shakin' Round" had been adapted to "Get Your Rights, Jack, and Don't You Stand Back No More." In a round of "I'm Gonna Sit at the Welcome Table," different members made up new verses, most of which were greeted by delighted laughter:

> I'm gonna be the first lady.
> I'm gonna be the first lady one of these days.
> I'm gonna be chief of police.
> I'm gonna work at Bell Telephone.
> I'm gonna go anywhere I want.
> I'm gonna marry the mayor's daughter. [This aroused great
> mirth.]

After the singing, a member reenacted a scene of violence at a bus station the previous summer. Great amusement was evoked by her version of one fellow leaping over a very high counter in his flight. This particular scene had obviously been reenacted and retold many times.

The talk then came back to the problems of the evening. Fear and distrust of the established Negro leaders on the negotiating team were freely expressed. Everyone felt that they, not the white merchants, might prove the real stumbling block to victory. The whites were, after all, the opponents. There was no need to worry about them; one knew where they stood. It was a clear-cut bargaining situation in which one tried to get the utmost advantage. As for the established Negro leaders, they might defeat everything by being too conciliatory and by trying to keep their radical young colleagues from using their power potential to the utmost.

Direct Action Tactics

In order to appreciate the barriers to unity in the Negro community, it is necessary to grasp the great sociological and philosophical differences that separate those individuals who work in a direct action group like CORE from those who participate in the more traditional groups that work through established, "institutionalized" political channels. The central difference between institutional and direct action lies in the mechanism through which decisions are influenced. "Mechanism" means the power that is mobilized and brought to bear on decision makers. Institutional political action revolves around the struggle for control over governmental bodies and public policy. Its pivotal instrument is the vote. In order to influence elections, groups that use institutional means must develop some type of broad consensus sufficient to give them numerical strength at the polls.* In the case of direct action, power lies in having an organization capable of inflicting financial loss on businessmen or creating disturbances and embarrassment for public officials. This may be accomplished by boycott, which requires a disciplined activist group plus fairly broad support in the Negro community, or by sit-ins that disrupt business or harm a firm's reputation; this tactic requires only small numbers of highly dedicated persons. This is essentially a process of coercion, although a certain amount of legitimation is necessary in order to persuade the majority and its political representatives to tolerate it. Such toleration may be achieved, however, far short of majority consensus on the changes brought about by the direct action.

CORE's two-year campaign to desegregate lunch counters in Southern City was a typical direct action campaign. The chapter was organized during the summer of 1960. Its first act was to send seven new members to a CORE training institute. In September the first sit-ins were held. Seven members sat-in at dime store A's all-white lunch counter. The police were called, but the store, obeying national company policy, refused to order the arrest of the demonstrators. After six hours of indecision on the part of police officials, the seven were arrested by order of the district attorney.

Some eight days later another small group sat-in at dime store B's lunch counter. This time they were arrested on the

---

* In devising these polar types, institutional and direct action, I have, of course, left out of account a very important intermediate area: lobbying and direct influence on government by business and other private institutions. Such strategies have not generally been available to Negroes or white integrationists in the South. Exclusion of this category of action is justified because our major interest is in comparing CORE with other Negro and white groups working toward similar ends in Southern City.

order of the management. Arrests of small groups for sitting-in, picketing, and handing out leaflets continued through December, when police stopped making arrests for mere picketing but ruled that picketing would be allowed only at the front entrances of the dime stores. They continued to interrogate pickets almost daily and for this purpose frequently took them to the police station. In April, dissatisfied because too few Negro customers could be kept out by front-door picketing alone and because they wanted greater publicity, the CORE group resumed back-door picketing. Five members were arrested.

Lunch-counter picketing and arrests continued throughout the eventful summer of 1961, at which time the publicity and fund-raising campaigns for the freedom riders were added to the picketing activities. Also, several cases of flagrant police brutality occurred during that summer: some directed at freedom riders in transit, some simply the customary brutality directed at individual Negroes. CORE protested these incidents by means of pickets and sit-ins at the police station and at city hall, and there were further arrests.*

During September, 1961, the police ordered CORE to stop all picketing activity for the two-week period during which schools were opening for their second integrated year. They ruled that picketing could be resumed thereafter but imposed a one-picket-per-store limitation. The chapter respected the need for a temporary cessation while schools were opening, but in November they were again picketing and sitting-in.

During December, mass student demonstrations at a Negro university, in which nearly 300 students were arrested, created great interest among Negro college students in Southern City. As a result of this heightened interest, the number of pickets and sit-in volunteers increased. Between December, 1961, and February, 1962, the number of participants varied from around twenty on weekdays to seventy on weekends. By this time

* During this two-year period, CORE lawyers handled over 350 arrests, though some of these were in connection with activities other than the lunch-counter demonstrations. Most of the cases, including one criminal-anarchy charge, were either dropped by the city authorities or never brought to trial. Eleven people were tried for various offenses and freed by the court; nine others were convicted and their cases reversed on appeal. On many occasions while awaiting trial, members served up to a week in "jail-without-bail" situations. The longest sentences served without appeal were two forty-five-day convictions.

police had abandoned the attempt to squelch the demonstrations by continuous arrests. Because CORE leaders did not feel they could finance legal actions and bail for such large numbers and did not trust most of the newcomers to serve out prison sentences, demonstrators, in order to prevent inciting the police to renewed arrests, were careful not to occupy whole counters.

Relaxation of police pressure, however, was offset by a heightening of other forms of harassment. Throughout the fifteen-month history of demonstrations, CORE members had frequently been tormented and sometimes physically assaulted by white citizens, often in full view of the police. But as long as the police appeared to be squelching the demonstrations, violence by individual whites remained somewhat in check. Now, because of the increased number of demonstrators and the relative inactivity of the police, violence by store personnel and onlookers increased greatly.

One CORE leader, in describing the conditions that prevailed from December through February, said that the sit-inners were threatened, assaulted by store personnel, and splashed with chemicals. Even a newsman was harassed, and policemen were rarely on the scene.

From the beginning of CORE's campaigning, Southern City's dime stores had been under pressure that resulted in serious economic losses at the national as well as at the local level. The original wave of sit-ins throughout the South in 1960 had inspired a long nationwide picketing campaign against these retail chains by CORE and other direct action groups. At its stockholders meeting in May, 1961, dime store A's president admitted that business during the past year had been "somewhat disappointing" as a result of desegregation problems.

The national publicity that accompanied the various incidents caused these companies great concern, but the incident that finally sparked active intervention by store A's national management was the severe beating of a white CORE demonstrator by two white men, one an employee. At this point Southern City CORE got in touch with the national chairman of CORE, who, together with a special representative of the company, came to Southern City to negotiate a temporary truce and to initiate negotiations for the simultaneous desegregation of lunch counters thoughout the city. On September 12, after nearly six months of negotiation, fifteen companies operating lunch-counter establishments and chains in the city desegregated their facilities.

Background of CORE Members

In the case of groups following an institutional political strategy, leaders are typically persons of prestige and power within the segment of the community they represent. They are also moderates in the sense that they are not drawn from the most extreme or militant portion of their constituency, but are close to the political position of the middle-roaders and the moderate wing of the opposing camp.

In the case of direct action, on the other hand, the activists are typically persons who are isolated from prestige and power within their own constituency and who represent the most radical and militant wing of their camp. This difference follows naturally from the fact that institutional leaders must win over to their camp the middle-roaders and moderates in the opposing camp, whereas activists must be persons who are sufficiently alienated from the prevailing consensus to risk condemnation and more serious sanctions resulting from a frontal, coercive attack on the opposition.

The membership of Southern City CORE fit the picture of a typical direct action group. There were about thirty members, fifteen of whom were part of the group's active nucleus. Of this nucleus, ten were college students, two were not working and were living at home during an interim in their studies, and three worked in semiskilled and service occupations. Most of the members' families had lived in Southern City for one or two generations. Except for two in white-collar jobs, the fathers of all the nucleus members were unskilled laborers. Most of the members, even two couples who were married and had children, lived with their parents. Typically, their home was a railroad flat composed of four or five rooms arranged in bead-string fashion without hallways. Furnishings were usually old and sparse. There were few rugs. The number of persons in a household ranged from six to ten or twelve. There were usually other grown siblings, who either attended college or worked, generally in white-collar jobs. Most of the mothers worked as domestic servants, waitresses, and the like. All the households that I visited gave the impression of having high morale and strong family organization. All were extremely neat and clean despite the poor quality of housing and furniture. In all these households the children, though frequently numerous, were making plans to move into white-collar and professional occupations.

Clearly then, these CORE members stemmed from the "upper lower" class within the Negro community's system of social stratification. Their parents were members of the unskilled but steady and respectable working class. The CORE members themselves were upwardly mobile, but still in an interim position where their future prospects did not yet accord them any real status of their own other than the nebulous one of being students.*

Another characteristic that defined CORE members as persons removed from positions of power and prestige was the age composition; all the members of the active nucleus were under twenty-five. The chairman was twenty-three and the two past chairmen were even younger, whereas almost all the "established" Negro leaders were middle-age.

During these two years of operation, the CORE chapter had only a handful of white members. There were four whites in the original group and about the same number in subsequent groups, but their turnover was very great. Of five former active white members on whom it was possible to gather information, two were undergraduate students at a "liberal-to-moderate" white college of high academic standing, two others were graduate students at the same college, and one was a professor at the state university. Three of the five were Northerners; the other two came from Border States. Parents'

* My findings disagree with those presented by Ruth Searles and J. Allen Williams, Jr., in "Negro College Students' Participation in Sit-Ins," *Social Forces*, Vol. 40 (March, 1962). In their analysis of 827 questionnaires distributed at three North Carolina colleges, the authors found that the students most active in the sit-ins were from slightly higher socioeconomic backgrounds than the least active group, though the results were not statistically significant. The discrepancy between the North Carolina observations and my data may be due to the fact that the sit-in movement had been very popular for a brief time in North Carolina. About 90 percent of the student sample polled had taken some part in the movement. Under these circumstances, it is more likely to be the college's established student leaders, usually from high socioeconomic backgrounds, who take the initiative, and only the social isolates remain uninvolved. My data are for hard-core activists who have been continuously involved for long periods and have "held the fort" between waves of popular enthusiasm. The social background characteristics of such a group would probably differ from those in the North Carolina case.

occupations ranged from skilled laborer to wealthy contractor.

Thus, although the Negro members of CORE were, by virtue of their background and age, truly outside of and isolated from the conservative influences of the elements of prestige and power in the Negro establishment, they did have roots within what may be termed the Negro masses: the great bulk of the city's Negro population. The white CORE members, on the other hand, were complete outsiders in the white community because they were all from outside the city and region and were unconnected with any segment of the white community except the academic subculture from which all of them were recruited.

Structure of CORE

Organizations geared to institutional political strategy typically emphasize a large membership with minimal participation by most members. The group is usually a typical secondary organization with loose, formally structured ties. In contrast, the ideal direct action group has a small, highly dedicated and involved membership united by strong primary-group ties. The reasons for this difference again follow from the central difference in the two strategies. A large, minimally involved membership is the best way to build up the widespread but relatively shallow commitment needed for numerical strength at the polls. Direct action, on the other hand, requires only small numbers of persons, but these must be so highly motivated and involved that they are willing to risk the great hardships involved in direct action.

Southern City CORE typified this generalization. In its internal structure, it was a cross between a political organization and a college friendship clique or neighborhood gang. On the formal side, there were five elected officers, an executive committee, and several operating committees. There were also regular weekly membership meetings, where all the members were entitled to discuss and vote on the group's business. The attendance at these meetings usually numbered around twenty people. However, the real work and day-to-day decision making was carried on by the active nucleus of officers plus a few other active members, all close personal friends who saw each other almost daily. Most active members reported that all their closest friends were in CORE, and although personal friendship was an important factor in binding the group together, it was the CORE bond, rather than any other common interest, that undergirded the relationships and loyalties of the group.

When CORE members got together, CORE business—past, present, and future—was virtually the only topic of conversation. CORE activities were so time consuming that most of the purely social activities occurred as by-products of CORE business: coffee after meetings, supper to discuss the newsletter, a party after a direct action project, or dropping over to discuss an impending action.

The active nucleus was a true primary group. Most members were emotionally "available" for such close ties because they were becoming independent of their parental households but had not yet established families of their own. More important, perhaps, the nature of direct action invariably bound the participants in close emotional ties. In the words of one CORE member: "We feel we are one family. We have the closeness of a family. We ran from the same things together. We've been implicated in the same things—we're constantly in touch with each other."

In terms of time spent in the group, then, to its active members CORE was truly a total-involvement organization. All those I queried said that they spent at least ten or fifteen hours a week on CORE activities. Some said that they spent almost every hour of their nonworking or nonstudying time in CORE. This is probably no exaggeration if we include the sociability interwoven with CORE activities. Only one member reported considerable involvement in another organization, and no member was more or even equally involved in any other activity. Beyond mere time commitment, it appeared that under the pressure of Southern conditions CORE usually became an overriding obsession with its members. One student who quit CORE to catch up on his graduate work reported:

It wasn't so much the time it took as the emotional involvement. I just couldn't stop thinking about it and start thinking about something else. We were having so much trouble organizing the community effectively that I would find myself always thinking of evolving strategy.

And another student said:

Since the arrest for handing out leaflets my whole life was covered with CORE. I suppose I spent almost every minute of my time involved in it. If I wasn't going to meetings I was talking to people here on campus. People would come up to me all the time if they wanted to know anything about what was going on. Everybody knew I was in it. My schoolwork went way down. I was continually on the spot. That's why I'm reluctant to go down there now and get into it again—because I know I'll get involved in it like this, totally.

In its isolation from other organizations, in the strong radicalism of its convictions, and in the semi-illegal nature of many of its activities, the group was bound by all of the forces that unite members of a political sect on the one hand and a juvenile gang on the other. But the negative features that become divisive in these other groups were counteracted by the peculiar combination of features in CORE. The powerlessness of the political sect, which results in a turning inward of hostilities in the form of philosophical disputes and heresies, was counteracted in CORE by the constant outlet for activity offered by direct action. The complete illegitimacy of a gang in the eyes of the outside world—and to a large extent in the eyes of its own members—results in the members fearing and resenting gang involvement at the same time that the condemnation of the outside world forces them further into the gang.[1] In CORE, on the other hand, the condemnation of the outside world could not be turned into resentment of the group because of the group's strong sense of moral legitimacy, a sense that was reinforced by the group's contacts with national CORE.

Relationship to White Community

Established Negro leaders whose organizations combine some forms of direct pressure with attempts to influence the white community and thus gain advantages for the Negro through institutional political action typically depend upon alliances with white liberal groups. They come into minimal contact with conservatives and archsegregationists. This pattern of persuasive contact underlies the weakness of such organizations because white liberals are few in number and lack real political and economic power. By contrast, the direct action group in the South engages in direct confrontations with conservative and segregationist power figures in both the political and the economic hierarchies of the city. The nature of this direct action contact is purely coercive and often violent. Contrary to the idealized version of direct action strategy as enunciated in the philosophy of nonviolence, there is no genuine attempt at communication, persuasion, or consensus building between these two conflicting groups. There is pushing and shoving and, eventually, bargaining, but there is no dialogue. Because the direct action strategy depends on coercion for its results, CORE groups have little tactical use for coalitions with white liberals, who may, at times, help to persuade the white community to initiate or accept reforms but who have little direct influence on the process of decision making.

If one observes the frequency and intensity of condemnation expressed by CORE members, it is obvious that the segregationist whites come in for less abuse from them, and less intensive abuse, than some factions within the Negro community. The white businessman, politician, policeman, heckler, or assailant was regarded as an enemy who had to be outmaneuvered, pressured, or at times endured. The threat posed by such people was treated as impersonally as one would treat a threatening natural phenomenon such as a flood or an earthquake.

This psychological distance was maintained even in the midst of direct physical confrontation or conflict because there were no positive expectations and no real attempt to communicate. Most of the comments made by CORE members about such people took the form of ridicule or mild mockery, accompanied by a tone of disbelief. These comments seemed to be intended mainly to reduce the stature of the enemy in order to lessen fear and discouragement. This joke, told at a CORE meeting, illustrates the kind of attitude expressed toward segregationists:

> These three big Negro guys went to the beach—this was just about the time when beaches were a big issue. So these two scrawny little white guys came up with bats in their hands. They stopped a ways off and looked at these big muscular Negro guys, and then one of them says to the other: "Should we take the chance that they're some of those nonviolent types?"

Criticism of the white community in general consisted of viewing whites as blind to the Negro's problems, irrational in their prejudices, hypocritical in their personal contacts with Negroes, dependent upon racist myths to cover exploitation and selfishness, and determined to impose racist values on Negroes. The real aim of these comments was to strip away the underpinnings of "white" values so that Negroes would stop respecting the white community. The members seemed also to be clarifying their own rejection of "white brainwashing" in order to strengthen their motivation for action.

The term "white power structure" was used frequently by CORE members. Its interpretation included business, community, and political leaders of the city. CORE comments about them were usually very specific and concerned individuals with whom CORE had negotiated or otherwise come in contact. Their general theme was that the power holders were moving too late and doing too little. Such comments served to keep alive the uncompromising spirit of the members; they pointed out that one could not be satisfied with whatever concessions have been or are being made. One comment, for example, was that "all this is being done a hundred years too late and would never have been done at all without our direct action."

CORE's contact with white liberals and moderates in Southern City was extremely minimal because Negro leaders were isolated from these people. Most of the white liberal groups were oriented toward influencing white opinion and putting pressure on political leaders. In this enterprise, support from Negro leaders could only weaken their position, and interracial memberships were considered politically impossible. One must add that, given the atmosphere in the city, social contact between Negroes and "respectable" whites was so difficult as to be almost nonexistent.

In the early 1960s the five organizations that were at various times involved in fighting racism ranged from liberal to moderate. For the CORE leadership, all of which was Negro, there were only two very indirect sources of contact with these groups. One was a white lawyer who had given legal aid to CORE and was also connected with two of the other groups, and the other was a Negro law firm that handled most of CORE's cases. Some of the Negro lawyers in this firm were acquainted with the head of another group and had participated in some meetings of the local human relations council. Several former white members had had contacts through their academic connections with faculty members who were active in the groups involved in other local civil rights issues. My interviews with CORE leaders and leaders of white liberal groups consistently showed that they did not even know each other's names and were unacquainted with the projects being carried out by the other organizations. At best, they knew of the existence of the other groups and of some past activities that had received wide newspaper publicity. The only white liberal group that had given any important help to CORE was one Unitarian church, which had donated sizable sums for legal defense. But this did not involve any close contact between the two parties. The donations had been worked out in a series of formal meetings between leaders of both organizations.

The absence of contact between CORE officials and white liberals was reflected in the attitudes of CORE members, who were neither hostile toward nor critical of white liberals; they were just indifferent. Because no help was really expected from the liberals, any support from them was regarded with pleased surprise. It is interesting to compare this attitude with those expressed in another study, in which "established" Negro leaders said that the white liberals were more dangerous to democracy than bigots, for at least bigots are honest.

When CORE's mildly negative reaction to white liberals is compared with the strongly negative reaction of the more conservative established Negro leadership, we suspect a difference not only in degree but in kind between the contacts and expectations that these two Negro groups had with respect to white liberals. Most non-CORE Negro leaders were very aware of, and concerned with, the constellation of white liberal and moderate groups because they counted on enlisting their cooperation and support for various projects and because they were interested in influencing the white public, though they were in a weak position to do so.

CORE, on the other hand, did not need such groups to carry out its strategy. Its direct action tactics automatically excluded it from gaining their support. But, more important, CORE was not basically concerned with influencing white public opinion through persuasion, education, or propaganda. It aimed directly at certain "power targets," such as businesses. The fact that the direct action campaign had some educational impact upon the white public was an inevitable by-product of the group's activities, and what was gained here did not require alliance with white liberal and moderate groups. In the context of this strategy the liberals were "counted out."

Relationship to Negro Community

Throughout its brief history in Southern City, the CORE chapter's contacts with established groups and leaders in the

Negro community were almost entirely negative, reflecting both a conflict of organizational interests and a clash of viewpoints.

In the late summer of 1960, when CORE was planning its first sit-in, the NAACP approached the group in the role of mediator between CORE, the mayor's office, and the dime store managers. The NAACP was motivated by its interest in peaceful school desegregation, which its legal actions had brought to a head and which was scheduled to begin in September. NAACP leaders promised to set up a negotiating session between CORE and the business leaders under the auspices of the mayor's office. At the negotiating session CORE representatives found that only the political authorities were present. The store managers had already been "talked to," and CORE was asked to hold off its picketing for a year in the interests of ensuring peaceful school integration. The group refused this proposition and voted to proceed with sit-ins immediately.

The next important contact with established Negro groups was in a newly formed organization set up in December, 1960. The organization was composed of about one hundred Negro leaders representing various groups in the Negro community, including CORE. During December, 1961, CORE had succeeded in getting the backing of some Negro churches, and a few ministers had actually joined the CORE picket lines to protest lunch-counter segregation. The leaders of the CORE chapter were trying, with some hope of success, to get the backing of this organization and of more Negro ministers.

But in January an event occurred that destroyed these small efforts at cooperation with a broader spectrum of Negro groups. The local Negro newspaper printed a bitterly worded letter in which CORE was accused of promoting interracial romances of the white male–Negro female variety, which have extremely unsavory overtones of concubinage in the Negro community. As a result of this letter, the ministers withdrew their support, and the newly formed organization decided to withhold its endorsement of the picketing.

The only interracial civil rights group in the city besides CORE was a human relations council. At the time of this study, the council had held only a few meetings. It was composed of the welfare-minded, rather impotent white liberals and a small group of "establishment" Negroes—all very light-skinned and obviously recruited from the highest echelons of the Negro community. The group was considering working on improving vocational and technical training in Negro high schools. CORE was invited to join it, but they sent only an occasional representative.

The CORE chairman's judgment on this council reveals the extent to which social class tensions affect the relations between CORE and established Negro leaders. Significantly, the negative reaction to the council was based solely on the character of the Negro members; the white members were completely ignored.

> At the human relations council—we've been asked to come to this kind of thing now, but we're out of place—we're strictly lowbrow. Most of us don't know how to act there, and, you know, we think different. M [the CORE group's lawyer] of course is an exception. His parents weren't middle class, but he's moved up, being a lawyer—although he doesn't belong to any of their social clubs because he thinks they're a bunch of phonies. Anyway, I don't think you can hope for much to come out of a group like that.

The various other Negro groups, the established Negro ministers, the so-called Negro leaders, the "black bourgeoisie," and the "old family group" all merged into a single category referred to by CORE members as the Negro establishment. This was the group against which CORE members expressed the most frequent, and by far the most vehement, hostility. These were CORE's real adversaries in the ideological struggle. For it was here, within the Negro community, that CORE engaged in its significant dialogues. Here, in battle against the relatively conservative and established groups, they attempted to create a new and more militant consensus of Negro opinion.

A fairly large proportion of CORE members had been recruited out of the NAACP Youth Council. Their defection to CORE resulted from their own belief in greater militancy, and they continued to resent the council as a roadblock to the growth of the direct action movement. One such member said of the council:

> They were always discussing their next party—or they are raising money to send delegates to the national convention. They are just social. They can't do anything that isn't approved by the adults. We used to always go asking them to help us picket. Once they came out—a couple of them. But they were never here when we needed them.

Another CORE member said of the established Negro leaders:

> Look, I'll give you an example of the way our so-called Negro leaders act. We asked them to picket the stores with us, so this thing would have more prestige. They refused—never a one came out. But when the city refused to let one of the nationally known integration leaders speak in the city auditorium they were all out there picketing—because they thought this was a big national thing and would be in all the newspapers.

The response of the established Negro leadership to CORE was equally vehement. One NAACP leader said:

> CORE groups have blackmailed Negro leaders all over the country. The attack which CORE has made has been equally vicious against segregation and the white leadership and the established Negro leadership. The NAACP has been pushed into the position of having to prove that it's liberal. We've lost membership in many places because of the way CORE has blackmailed us and pushed us. After all we can't come out in opposition to CORE—we're afraid to come out in opposition to them.

There were some groups and factions within the Negro community with which CORE had, at various times, a cooperative relationship. Shortly after its founding, CORE approached the NAACP Youth Council for help in picketing. For a brief period at the height of the demonstrations in the winter of 1961, about fifty Youth Council members did participate. However, most of the time, the sole result of CORE's approaches to the Youth Council was that the most militant members of the council went over to CORE and quit their activities with the council. These defecting members, with the air of amused, contemptuous onlookers, would occasionally return to sit in on Youth Council meetings. Feelings were not very warm on either side. In the judgment of members who left the Youth Council to join CORE, it was usually the children of white-collar and professional parents who refrained from participating in direct action because of strong parental objections. Children from working class families were more apt to join because such parental pressures did not exist.

A more positive relationship was established between CORE and a consumers' group, which had been founded a few months before the CORE chapter and was composed largely of working class persons in their forties and fifties.

The consumers' group was dedicated to gaining improved employment opportunities through the picketing and boycotting of stores in Negro areas, and these actions were quite successful. During the first two years of its operations, it claimed credit for having secured more than 150 white-collar jobs for Negroes. On a number of occasions CORE helped this group by joining its picket lines.

During the winter of 1961 the large and dramatic student demonstrations at a Southern university created a good deal of feeling on Southern City's Negro campuses. CORE led several sympathy demonstrations in Southern City, and about forty students thereafter swelled the ranks of the CORE sit-inners at local dime store lunch counters. Student participation from the city's Negro campuses was in exact inverse relationship to their academic standing and the average socioeconomic level of their student bodies. The school with the highest academic and socioeconomic level provided few demonstrators and generally supplied few active CORE members. The school with the second highest level occupied an intermediate position, and the school lowest on both counts supplied the largest number of demonstrators and active CORE members.

That this ratio was again largely due to the effect of negative pressure by middle class parents is suggested by the CORE chairman's comments on the reactions of parents to their children's arrests during the sympathy demonstrations:

> Few of the kids from the wealthier cliques participated. Those that did—well, it happened so fast that the parents didn't have time to try and stop them. They weren't in touch with their parents beforehand. Some of these parents performed awfully. They came down and said, "You're disgracing us, going to jail." To them going to jail is a badge of disgrace. They can't distinguish between going to jail for this and going to jail for some crime. Most of the working parents—like with the CORE members—just object to the nonviolence. That's what they disapproved of most. They wished we were taking guns.

While the Negro establishment represented a competitor for the leadership of the Negro community, CORE had to draw for its members and supporters on the average Negro, whose thinking it hoped to reshape. CORE's disappointment with its constituency was reflected by a fairly high incidence of unfavorable comment. The criticisms were mainly that the average Negro was too cowardly to stand firm, too brainwashed by the white culture, and too apathetic to support the militant movement. Although these comments were occasionally very bitter, as when members recalled how Negroes crossed their picket lines or slammed doors in their faces during voter registration drives, they were often tinged with understanding and humor. There was a sense that "this is the sad condition from which we have just emerged ourselves." This story, told at a CORE gathering, illustrates this attitude:

> We were going through some small town on the bus and we saw this Negro lady walking along the street—and there were nothing but whites around her—and Alice yells out the window, "Hey, lady, are you a New Negro or an Old Negro?" and the lady scrunches herself all up and says, "I'm an ooooold Negro!"

Attitudes toward Black Muslims were almost equally divided between favorable and unfavorable. Muslims had one temple in the city but were not very strong. However, CORE members had considerable contact with them because they moved in the two strata where Muslims make their greatest impact: lower class groups and student groups. CORE members reported frequent conversations with Muslim members and sympathizers and had invited a Muslim speaker to one of their meetings. In the struggle to radicalize the Negro community, Muslims were seen more as allies than as competitors. Like CORE, they were trying to undo white brainwashing and to undermine the prestige of the middle class Negro leadership. They were admired for their dramatic exposure of racist myths and for their ability to appeal to lower class Negroes. Although Muslims were criticized for their "inverse racism" and their goal of a segregated society, these criticisms were not usually very vehement.

The commitment to interracial groups was the one radical value of national CORE that conflicted directly with the inclination of the lower class Negro community and the black nationalists. This was also the one radical value that was most expendable to Negro leaders of Southern City's CORE, as was indicated by the reaction of Negro members to the letter in which the local Negro paper criticized CORE members for interracial dating. The article, as will be recalled, injured CORE's position in negotiations for support of picketing with other Negro groups. These events precipitated a crisis within the group: white members insisted that interracial socializing was central to CORE's goals, while most Negro members felt that this was peripheral and expendable if it hurt the group's standing in the Negro community. As a result of this dispute most white members left the group.

CORE's cooperative or relatively sympathetic contacts in the Negro community suggest that the direct action movement, although largely a generational phenomenon, is also very closely tied to social class. Within the student generation, it was, as we have seen, the students from working class homes who most frequently participated. On the other hand, cooperation and understanding between CORE and the consumers' group was great despite the age difference, largely because the consumers were a working class group. Membership in the Muslims is young and predominantly lower class, and both of these characteristics—youth and lower class status—tend to isolate the individual from contact with, and sympathy for, the prestige and power structure of the Negro and white communities.

Struggles for Consensus Within the Negro Community

Throughout CORE's campaign to desegregate lunch counters, members of white churches and moderate organizations summarily condemned the direct action, and reaction among Negro leaders was mixed. The leading white daily newspaper at first refused to cover the arrests and later covered them too thoroughly, giving names and addresses of those arrested. All the editorial comment was negative.

The decision to negotiate desegregation of the lunch counters did not stem from any liberalization of local white public opinion or from any change of policy on the part of white political leaders. The initiative for bringing about the negotiations between storeowners and Negro leaders stemmed, rather, from the nationwide chain stores, which feared the economic losses and adverse publicity of the demonstrations on a national level.* Thus, a small nucleus of fifteen to thirty persons plus a temporary following of perhaps forty more—all lacking prestige or influence in the existing leadership structure of the city, but all armed with the willingness to expose themselves to arrest, violence, and condemnation—had, over the course of two years, created a completely new bar-

---

* During the Southern sit-in movement of the previous summer, these chains had suffered financially from disruption in their Southern stores and from sympathy boycotts of their Northern outlets.

gaining position. This bargaining position was so strong that conservatives in the white business community were willing to deal with them and insisted on dealing first and foremost not with "influential Negroes" but with "whoever can stop these demonstrations."

To this point, CORE consistently appeared as a direct action group organizing coercive strength against the white community while engaging in little communication with them. Within its own racial community, CORE allied itself with other youthful and lower class groups while carrying on its ideological struggle against the established, older, middle class Negro leadership. Yet at the point where CORE was asked to enter into negotiations with white merchants, it suddenly began to play a new role that appeared to contradict the picture developed earlier. Although the merchants had made it clear that they only wanted to talk with the groups responsible for the direct action, CORE invited the established Negro leaders to join the Negro negotiating team.

Thus, they brought in the very establishment that they so greatly opposed ideologically: leaders of moderate Negro groups, leaders of Negro churches, and the publisher of the Negro paper. CORE had only two persons on the seventeen-member team: the chairman of the chapter and one of the lawyers connected with CORE, who served as chairman of the entire Negro negotiating team. Why, just when it had created an independent bargaining position, did CORE bring in these other elements?

A partial reason lies in the fact that the cooperation of these persons was needed. The editor of the Negro newspaper was brought in to prevent publicity leaks. Both Negro and white members were afraid that news of the negotiations might encourage the White Citizens Council to organize countermoves. The consumers' group, which had been picketing intermittently for jobs, had to be brought into the agreement in order to put an effective moratorium on all demonstrations during the course of the negotiations. To bring in their representatives was not enough; CORE leaders felt that they should also bring in two established Negro leaders who controlled the consumers' group's funds and could better influence its conduct.

However, these reasons do not seem sufficient to account for the large amount of power that was literally given away by the group. They were presented as explanations for a decision that the CORE leaders did not themselves fully understand. During the course of the six-month negotiations, CORE negotiators were frequently infuriated because they felt that they were being held up and sabotaged more by their fellow Negroes than by the whites sitting across the table. Yet they continued to defend the necessity of having included "the Negro power structure" in the negotiations.

Actually the decision seemed to stem largely from an unwillingness to take power because of the low status of the CORE members within the Negro community. A revealing quotation from one CORE leader reflects this lack of confidence:

> The merchants never said who should be on the Negro negotiating team. We could have had seventeen CORE members on it if we had wanted to, but we had to get broad representation. The only thing the merchants were interested in was that they were talking to the right people—that is, the people who could stop the demonstrations. We had to get the other because we were vis-à-vis the power structure of the whole community, not just dealing with the merchants on the main street. The Chamber of Commerce was involved, and many prominent persons like bank presidents. So we had to have the power people in the Negro community.

In CORE's invitation to the established Negro leaders we see the organization in an unfamiliar role: as compromiser and consensus builder. The established Negro leaders lived in a defined situation that included white prestige figures (and indeed the white community) among their reference groups. Just as this relationship inclined these leaders to trade away part of their power position for the good opinion of the white leadership, so the CORE leaders—cut off from the white leadership by a great gulf of class, age, and ideology, and hence quite unwilling to give way to them—inevitably had to include within their defined situation the established Negro leadership simply as a reference group. They, too, had to trade away part of their power position in return for the prestige and sense of security they borrowed from the endorsement of established leaders.

Within the Negro community, then, CORE's role, despite the harsh aspect of its ideological attacks on the established Negro leadership, was, at times, a consensus-building one in its attempts to organizationally and ideologically mobilize its own "side" for attack on the white community. Vis-à-vis the white community, it played a wholly radical role in that it used power against white targets without real attempt at legitimation. Through the coercive power generated by direct action, the burden of adjustment to an unwanted situation was shifted from the Negro community to the white community.

Were CORE the only element at work in such a situation, the result would be a rapid breakdown of consensus and order in the entire community. However, it has generally been noted that direct action sets off new processes within the white community that prevent the complete breakdown of consensus. Liberal and moderate groups suddenly emerge and try to readjust the white community to the changing circumstances. At the same time, established Negro leaders, pushed from behind by the young radicals and encouraged by the emergence of the white liberals, take a stronger tone in their attempt to reeducate the white community. Both elements are able to emerge under the "cover" provided by the extreme radicalism of direct action, in other words, as a lesser evil. Within this process, the breakdown of the consensus-building mechanisms and the development of an acute Negro-white polarization remains a constant and threatening possibility.

NOTE

1. For a discussion of the group's legitimacy as it applies to the delinquent subculture, see Albert K. Cohen, *Delinquent Boys: The Culture of the Gang* (New York: Free Press, 1955), pp. 67–69.

CHAPTER 7

Meaning of Nonviolence
for the Rank and File

How did the rank-and-file CORE activist feel about the doctrine and practice of nonviolence? What differences in depth and quality of commitment existed between the Northern and Southern members, white and Negro members, and lower class and middle class members? Answers to these questions are partially provided from an analysis of forty-six extensive interviews with active CORE members throughout the country. The breakdown of these interviews by race and region is as follows:

SOUTH		NORTH	
Negro	*White*	*Negro*	*White*
16	7	12	11

Other answers emerge from materials gathered at meetings and during participant observation in official as well as informal activities of various groups.

The respondents' attitudes toward nonviolence in the civil rights movement can be divided into four broad types:

1. *Accepting nonviolence as a moral commitment.* Nonviolence was seen as a moral imperative and as an inescapable commitment for the movement. For example: "Violence has never accomplished anything and turning to violence would destroy the movement"; "I reject the idea of vengeance or stooping to the same methods as the enemy."

2. *Accepting nonviolence as a technique only.* The respondent emphasized that he considered nonviolence a technique rather than a moral commitment but did not entertain the possibility of other methods. For example: "Nonviolence is the best technique because it makes the best impression and wins us allies"; "It's the best way to keep the law on our side."

3. *Questioning nonviolence.* The respondent accepted nonviolence under present circumstances but might prefer violence in the future or under some circumstances. For example: "The violence in Birmingham at least forced everybody to realize the extent of the problem"; "Unfortunately, violent self-defense isn't possible now because we are too weak."

4. *Rejecting nonviolence.* For example: "Nonviolence is our greatest hindrance in the South"; "It is just another way of letting Negroes get kicked around"; "Only violence will make the whites back down and stop using it against us."

In attitudes toward nonviolence the distribution of the forty-six respondents among these categories was:

1.	Moral commitment to nonviolence	30%
2.	Commitment to nonviolence as a technique	24
3.	Questioning of nonviolence	24
4.	Rejection of nonviolence	11
5.	Don't know, no answer	11

The data indicated less adherence to nonviolence than might have been inferred from a perusal of CORE literature or from observation at the staff-led training institute. Those who supported nonviolence on some basis outnumbered those who questioned or rejected it, but they did not, by any means, constitute an overwhelming majority: 54 percent as against 35 percent.

Among those who did support nonviolence, how much depth of conviction and intellectual preparation did we find? Only seven Southern respondents and an equal number of Northern respondents reported having read anything beyond CORE leaflets on the subject of nonviolence. The main works that had been read were Martin Luther King's *Stride Toward Freedom,* Louis Fischer's *Biography of Gandhi,* and some of Gandhi's own writings on nonviolence. Three of the fourteen respondents who had read this material were among those rejecting nonviolence.

Only four respondents indicated that they considered nonviolence a personal ethic or "way of life" as well as something to be followed in the movement. Two of these four did not appear to have enough intellectual understanding to have applied the ethic to themselves in anything resembling the spirit in which it was understood by Gandhi, Martin Luther King, and other exponents. In both cases the investigator had occasion to observe that the respondents did not, in fact, adhere to a spirit of nonviolence when off the direct action line.

There were only two respondents in the entire sample who could be classified as "nonviolent absolutists," in that they had a fairly extensive and coherent intellectual understanding of the theory of nonviolence: they felt that the integration movement had a moral commitment to nonviolence; they were thoroughgoing pacifists with regard to war; and they seriously attempted to practice nonviolence as a personal ethic.

A closer look at these two respondents provides rather interesting information. One was a deeply religious young white Northerner who took a Christian pacifist position on all issues. He worked as a laborer and lived in voluntary poverty while pursuing his real interest: the ministry of a small Universalist church. The respondent described Universalism as a non-denominational Christian faith that transcends class, race, and creed and has very strong emphasis on social action. He found the United States highly objectionable because of its racism and militarism and its general materialism and reliance on coercion and force. His religiously grounded pacifism attracted him to CORE, but he was a peripheral member and felt dissatisfied with the organization because of its lack of serious philosophical commitment. He preferred working through his church or through various pacifist groups to which he belonged.

The other nonviolent absolutist was a forty-year-old Northern Negro who had been in CORE since the early 1940s. He was the only respondent who had been a member this long and for whom CORE had become a major and lifelong influence. He came to CORE as a violent and angry young man and was won to a position of classic nonviolence through association with an early CORE chapter that had been composed largely of white pacifist intellectuals. As part of his philosophical development, he left his traditional church and became a member of the liberal-humanist Ethical Culture Society. This respondent also felt alienated from the CORE chapter currently operating in his city. He compared the new "businesslike" attitude toward direct action with the more philosophical and purist approach of the 1940s:

> We would refer to the philosophy when we had decisions to make. For example, at the sit-in someone had a Bible with them

and accidentally left it in their place as if to save the place and no one would take that seat. Well, next meeting it was suggested we save seats next to us this way. We discussed whether this was in keeping with the philosophy for three hours. Some felt it was trickery. The vote was very close and came out in favor of using it—but we didn't use it because the vote had been so close. We always wanted unanimity on what we did.

In contrast to this man's experience, most respondents had joined CORE between 1959 and 1962. They had come into chapters that were expanding very rapidly as a result of the sit-in movement and the freedom rides. They were young, predominantly Negro, and far more interested in attaining the goal of Negro equality than in guarding the nonviolent purity of the means.

Most of the respondents who declared themselves in favor of nonviolence showed an amazing naïveté about the philosophical implications of the method. They frequently described nonviolence as a way of outwitting the enemy and took vindictive pleasure in the embarrassment and confusion into which the method could force an unprepared opponent. Respondents frequently explained that they approved of nonviolence because "it confuses whites" and "they don't know how to handle it."

Although the theory of nonviolence suggests that the enemy may be converted partly as a result of the surprise or "moral jujitsu" element of the tactic, the spirit of these remarks is far afield from the attitude demanded of demonstrators by nonviolent philosophy. That attitude was voiced by one lone respondent who described the strategy from a genuinely nonviolent point of view:

> The whites in the South know how to handle violence—they are used to it. But if we just sit there and smile, he doesn't know how to react. And if you sit there and love him—I hope you would love him or at least be sympathetic—well, he doesn't know how to react, and maybe eventually he will forget he is white and you're a Negro and start smiling with you—just men.

Image of Lower Class Negro Violence

Like adherents of all social movements, Negro CORE members turned to the movement for the solution of pressing personal problems caused by the racial situation.[1] Primary among these problems was that of self-hatred. There is a need to overcome the negative self-image that American society forces on every Negro. Reaction to the nonviolent doctrine and technique was strongly influenced by its effect on the member's self-esteem. Ambivalence on this subject is based on the fact that nonviolence had both a potentially positive and a potentially negative effect on the Negro self-image. On the one hand, physical violence and verbal abuse are part of the negative stereotype of lower class Negro behavior, and nonviolence provided an attractive alternative for those trying to overcome this image. On the other hand, the image of the Negro as passive and cowardly also haunted the members, and certainly this was a trait that the movement was particularly anxious to change. Strength and militancy were terribly important to Negro CORE members, and given the basic assumptions of American culture, it was extremely difficult to cast these characteristics within a nonviolent mold.*

The image of lower class violence held an immediate threat for Negro CORE members because most of them either were in the process of moving up into the middle class or had made such a shift in the recent past. Fifteen of the twenty-eight Negro respondents came from homes in which fathers or guardians were poor farmers or unskilled or semiskilled workers; five had fathers who were skilled workers; and three had fathers who were ministers or who combined the ministry with farming.† Only four respondents came from homes that were genuinely middle class, with fathers in professional or proprietary positions.‡ In contrast, eight of the respondents were already established in professional, proprietary, or white-collar occupations and eleven were college students preparing themselves for such occupations. Of the remaining nine, three were skilled workers and five were in miscellaneous categories somewhere between lower and middle class (a well-paid custodian with a college degree, a small, low-income proprietor, and so on). Only one respondent, a service worker

* First we shall focus only on Negro reactions to the conflicting pressure of these two images. White members, as we shall see later, generally adopted Negro members as their major reference group. They tended to take their cue from Negro members and often developed vicarious reactions to Negro identity problems on the basis of their familiarity with the attitudes of the Negro members.

† In all cases, these ministerial positions involved only a slightly higher education and income than that of farmer or unskilled worker. They did, however, indicate a somewhat higher social status.

‡ Information on the father's occupation was missing in one case.

with an eighth-grade education, resembled the low status of the parent generation.

The Negro CORE member, who was in the process of shedding his lower class identity but was exposed to violent situations in the course of his direct action activity, found in the nonviolent doctrine and role assurance against lapses into a type of behavior that was both dangerous and degrading in its status implications. One Southern respondent clearly expressed the connection between his own upward mobility and his acceptance of nonviolence within the movement:

> Once you're in CORE I think nonviolence should be practiced during the movement and at other times. I was a gang fighter and pretty violent when I was young. When I came to college I realized that this way you don't accomplish anything. After a semester at school and joining the movement I had changed. I had thought about it, "Why should I fight?" I guess partly I was just growing up.

Another young respondent used the idea of nonviolence to dissociate himself from lower class behavior on the part of relatives with whom he lived:

> I believe in it as a way of life. Everyone should practice it—not get into fights. If someone swings at you and you don't swing back, he'll be sorry in the end. I have eight brothers and nephews and sometimes at home violence is at hand, but it's put a change in my attitude. I always stay away from trouble.

One respondent remarked explicitly on the connection between nonviolence and the negative stereotype of lower class violence:

> I am very much in favor of nonviolence. Again, this is the Negro stereotype—that Negroes all carry weapons. Nonviolence proves that their convictions are definitely wrong. They see that only bad or ignorant Negroes would carry these things. Then they have these impressions that we smell and dress nasty. Well, we negotiate in a well-dressed manner and we aren't offensive. That gets at their belief that we don't know how to act.

Within this context of middle class versus lower class behavior, nonviolence was frequently understood simply as "acting intelligently" and "reasoning things out" rather than as indulging in epithets and fisticuffs. Our former gang member says of his previous associates, "Most of them just fight because someone hollered at them. If they would discuss it in a pleasant tone of voice, they could work it out."

The greatest triumph, of course, came when the Negro CORE member "outclassed" the white segregationist by his nonviolent "manners." One respondent reported that when he was arrested "the Sergeant hollered at me and I asked him quietly not to holler and we could both understand each other better. He changed his manner and stopped hollering . . ."

Half of the respondents whose fathers were skilled workers, ministers, proprietors, or professionals questioned or rejected nonviolence, while only a fifth of those whose fathers were in low-status occupations took this position. Respondents from higher-status homes felt less immediately threatened by the image of lower class violence, and their greater self-confidence made them generally more unwilling to apologize to the white community for supposed negative traits. We found the relationship between the father's occupational status and the Negro CORE member's willingness to question or reject nonviolence to be as follows:

	Skilled Workers, Ministers, Professionals, Proprietors	Farmers, Domestics, Unskilled and Semiskilled Workers
Persons accepting nonviolence* as moral commitment or technique	6	12
Persons questioning or rejecting nonviolence	6	3

* Due to the small number of cases, the four categories of nonviolent commitment used previously have been collapsed into two.

Image of Negro Passivity

The pressure to reject nonviolence arises from the desire to overcome the negative image of Negro passivity and from the psychological difficulties involved in the repression of hostile reactions to aggression. These pressures found different expression in the North and South. The typical Southern member's response was to support the nonviolent commitment on an ideological level, while expressing his ambivalence in various indirect ways. Off the direct action line and outside the context of philosophical discussion, members frequently indulged in vicarious violence. In the following jokes, told at a Southern chapter meeting, the Negro's supposed tendency toward violence is openly relished:

There was this big Negro sitting in the bus station in McComb, Mississippi, and a white guy comes up to him and just slaps him silly—till his eyeballs turn around—and the Negro turns the other cheek. So the guy slaps him around even worse till the guy's brains are all jarred up. But he just sits there and doesn't say anything. Finally, the white guy spits at him, and then the Negro reaches in his pocket (this is reenacted—the Negro is very cool and quiet, he draws out a razor), and he says, "I've just got to cut you a *little* bit."

This big, muscular Negro was sitting on a bus and a white man told him to move to the rear, and he said, "Un-uh, I'm not moving." So then the white man told him he was going to ask the bus driver to make him move. The Negro said, "All right, but before you do that, I think I should tell you something. I'm not one of those nonviolent Negroes."

Anecdotes in which members recalled hostile acts against whites "before I became nonviolent" were received with great tolerance and amusement. Members often seemed totally unaware of the inconsistencies that their ambivalence toward nonviolence created in their thinking. One respondent, who generally voiced the strongest opposition to the use of physical coercion, proudly described his city as one in which

Negroes are close to each other. When violence occurs they stand up for each other. I've heard where in other towns if a guy gets knocked down on the next block, they'll just walk away. Here, they're known to fight back. That's why the tension here isn't high. Negroes will walk anywhere in town without fear.

A chairman of a Southern CORE group, who generally supported nonviolence, told with satisfaction about the time he was sitting-in at a lunch counter and a white woman got up because he had sat down:

I announced that I hadn't come down to sit next to her—that she was as repulsive to me as vice versa—and that I had just come to eat. I had everybody in the place laughing at her and she left the place crying.

The ambivalence that the two opposing negative images—lower class violence and cowardly passivity—created with regard to nonviolence is shown in the fact that about half of the Southern respondents remarked that before they got into their first nonviolent direct action they fully expected that they would hit back, yell back, or otherwise lose their self-control. Yet most of them reported that "surprisingly" they had no difficulties at all in controlling themselves. The fact that most members experienced little difficulty in maintaining nonviolent discipline might be attributed, in part, to the very passivity that they were striving to overcome. The reported anticipation of difficulty was a disclaimer of this trait.

Rejection of Nonviolence in Northern Chapters

In contrast to the ambivalent attitude in the Southern chapters, Northern Negro CORE members were more positive in their rejection of nonviolence. Northern leaders frequently reported that nonviolence was not an issue for them and that they considered it unimportant and uninteresting:

> Nonviolence is a nonissue here. We go over the *Rules for Action* when we picket. We have an information session for inexperienced people and we just rattle them out. We tell them not to answer nasty comments, but it's really very minor.

When Northern members discussed the problem of nonviolence they generally thought in terms of the South.* Many saw violence as a distinct possibility and were very realistic in their assessment of the naked power factors involved in the situation:

> In these situations where demonstrators are kicked around by whites, I believe in cases like that—where the white people would allow their kids to come out there and heckle these people—they'll do that if they know you're nonviolent. But if they know you're not nonviolent and they may get killed, well, they'd keep their kids home, because people think of themselves. Take the Muslims—they preach they believe in violence, so they say—and so the average white, well, he tells his kids, "Don't go round those guys."

Another Northern respondent, who was raised in the South, similarly appraised the white man as reacting solely to force:

> In some sections of the South violence would help. You know, there have been Negroes in the South who have never been mistreated because they were violent and would defend themselves and shoot somebody who bothered them, and the whites would brand them crazy and tell each other, "Don't bother him!" . . .

* The interviews were completed before the major outbreaks of rioting in the urban North, beginning with the Harlem riot in 1963.

If the white man in the South loses his sense of protection, then I think you can talk with him.

Some of the most militant Northern members, however, openly rejected nonviolence for themselves because of the implication of passivity, which they found unbearable. One member explained why he felt dissatisfied when picketing:

> There is a begging aspect of it I don't like. When I am walking out in front of a store I am essentially saying to people that I'm a Negro and Negroes are not treated well—will you please do something about it? I don't want to see myself quite like that —it's hard to find the words to use. I would rather see myself standing forth a man like any man and making certain I receive my due—nothing plaintive—no asking. When I am walking in front of a realtor's office, I still feel I am begging him. I would feel better if I could just walk in and shove him out of the way and look at the listings—that, I would feel, would be being a man.

Another respondent rejected nonviolence for the same reasons when he said:

> I feel now that if another Negro struck me, I could walk off and not strike him—because I'd feel that nothing could be gained by it. But, if a white man did it, I couldn't, because he would be inferring more than his battery against me. I mean the meaning of it would run deeper.

In the Southern chapters, members alternated between the support of nonviolence as an effective moral appeal to the enemy and the expression of hostility vicariously or in the form of occasional breaches of nonviolent behavior on or off the direct action line. In Northern chapters, covert expressions of hostility and actual breaches of nonviolent discipline rarely occurred. This absence was due to the more solidly middle class composition of these chapters—including the higher percentage of middle class whites—and to their less frequent exposure to violent provocation. On a philosophical level, however, nonviolence was more frequently questioned by Northerners. For example, they were more willing to admit that direct action worked through direct financial pressure, rather than through the vaunted method of moral suasion; and open argument in favor of legitimating the use of defensive violence occurred much more frequently in the North than in the South. Typical of this openly aggressive attitude was the comment of this member:

The thing I like best about CORE is when we get really well organized and really smash the enemy. It's always amazing how much more cooperative these businessmen are when they've been losing money for a while. I've never seen any changing of hearts. I'm very cynical about that.

Nonviolence and the "Militant Activist" Image

The negative and positive implications of nonviolence, in terms of the Negro member's self-image, determined the peculiar way in which nonviolence was incorporated into the role of the Negro militant. In order to soften its passive-cowardly implications, nonviolence was expressly linked with courage, militancy, discipline, and selfless devotion to the cause. One respondent, after describing a local leader as a "real Gandhian," elaborated by saying:

He would give his money when the kids needed it. He quit his job and schooling for the movement. He put the movement before his own wife and children. It's not the speech-making that impresses, but this absolute sincerity.

Heroism, determination, and the power stemming from disciplined and united action were combined in this account of one member's first direct action encounter:

I took seventeen high school kids to the theater on A Street. When the manager saw me, he was trembling, but he was indignant. I was the first one at the window and he didn't know the others were behind me. He refused me and I thought, "There are seventeen in back of me and this is CORE." He called the police and they came out there and preached to the kids, "It's obvious the manager doesn't want you here and you-all go home." I let him finish and then I said, "Have you finished?" And then I told the kids, "Get back in that line," and they got in just like soldiers. And the people stood around saying, "Look at them, they're not afraid of the police." It's just a joy to talk about it. Later, when we got ready to go home for the night, the captain said to me, "I hope you're not coming back—you shouldn't come back." And I just looked at him quietly and said, "If they send me back, I'll be back."

The same basic emotions were expressed by another respondent who described a mass march and tear gas attack as "the most gratifying experience of my life." He told about several thousand students who marched to the city jail in support of a small group that had been arrested:

When we had all arrived we started singing "We Shall Overcome" and after we finished there was a peaceful quiet, like I've never heard before in my whole life. We stood there, the police stood there, and the white mob stood there—we all just stood there. And then, in the background, faintly we heard the students in the jail sing to us. We couldn't see them but they chanted, "Oh students don't you weep don't you mourn." It brought tears to my eyes. Even now as I talk about it I can feel chills running up and down my spine.

The singing was followed by a police charge, and the respondent recalls:

I saw one little girl—weighed about seventy pounds—and the policeman gave the command for a dog to leap at her. And one of the basketball players—a great big boy—put himself in front of her. The dog leaped and came back down with his suit and all his clothes torn off and the boy just smiled and walked off. I saw beauty that day.

During the tear gas attack the respondent was temporarily blinded by a bomb that hit him in the chest. He continued:

When I was able to see again I saw some of the girls getting themselves together. Some went back to the campus in an ambulance; they had been hit in the legs with nightsticks. And all of them—their clothes were torn and they were many of them bleeding—they were all standing in line again. In that few minutes they had pulled themselves back together and they were singing as loud as they could, "I'm gonna sit at the welcome table." And the police stood there and didn't say a word.

On a day-to-day level, nonviolence appeared to the members to be part of the set procedure of investigation, negotiation, demonstration, and civil disobedience as outlined in the *CORE Rules for Action* and as taught at regional and national CORE workshops. This set procedure made the member feel expert and secure in the possession of a standardized and proved method of conducting campaigns. Nonviolence was here merged with concepts of orderliness and discipline. For example, to most members the practice of having one spokesman make all decisions and handle all public statements during an action project was part of "nonviolent discipline." The rule against answering hecklers, the standardized procedure for protecting oneself during physical assault, and the rule that if anyone loses self-control he must leave the scene of action were all combined to give the demonstrator a well-defined and firmly structured role in the midst of an often dangerous and chaotic situation.

Thus, nonviolence became part of a new image that combined the ideas of direct action procedure, militancy, orderliness, discipline, and unity with the idea of abstaining from verbal and physical abuse. Nonviolence was so merged in this larger image that respondents frequently mistook the question "Do you think nonviolence is effective?" to mean "Do you think direct action is effective?" The new role provided an alternative to both passivity and sporadic violence. One respondent explicitly recognized the extent to which these two traits are really opposite sides of a coin and asserted the efficacy of the new alternative:

> Nonviolence was a very new idea to me. I thought it was a good idea—that we should be determined and know exactly what we are doing and not let anything ruffle us. People have this idea of the Negro as shuffling his feet and "I'll pull a knife on you." These are opposite qualities, but they go together. You are supposed to be retarded, or almost—at any rate, very slow. But, if you can't stand it any more, you pull a knife.

In the setting of this new syndrome, the more inward qualities of nonviolence, such as genuine goodwill toward the enemy, were de-emphasized. The philosophical foundations of nonviolent philosophy that assert the primacy of means over goals were similarly ignored.* The way in which nonviolence was embedded in the image of militancy and discipline made it a source of temporary support for nonviolence as well as a potential method for undermining it. For the moment, association with militancy and direct action in-

---

* At the heart of every genuine pacifist philosophy is the assertion of the absolute primacy of means over ends. Gandhi advised his followers to abandon all attachment to goals that might tempt them away from the purity of their means: "When there is no desire for fruit, there is no temptation for untruth or *Himsa*. Take an instance of untruth or violence, and it will be found that at its back is the desire to attain the cherished end" (Gandhi, *Yeravda Mandir;* quoted in Joan Bondurant, *Conquest of Violence* [Princeton: Princeton University Press, 1958], p. 116). This aspect of nonviolence has been played down by Martin Luther King, who evades the problem by assuming that nonviolence will always be the best strategy for attaining civil rights. It has been more clearly understood and accentuated by the early CORE groups but was seldom mentioned or discussed after 1961.

creased the attractiveness of nonviolence. However, under pressure toward increasing radicalism, it became easy to emphasize other parts of the image to the virtual exclusion of the nonviolent component. As a result, the abandonment in 1966 of the doctrine of nonretaliation did not appear to most Negro CORE members as a fundamental change in their role as civil rights activists.

Moderate-Radical Determinant of Nonviolent Commitment

If support for nonviolence was not grounded in any deep or consistent pacifist philosophy, what was the origin and meaning of this commitment? The type of violence under discussion here was exclusively self-defensive, that is, violence in situations where public law and order did not function. Only one respondent advocated the use of violence in the absence of immediate provocation, and then only against clearly violent groups like the Klan. What was here being forsworn, therefore, was a type of self-defense that was traditionally sanctioned in American society. Given the absence of any general pacifist commitment, the suspicion necessarily arises that nonviolence in CORE was an expression of ideological conservatism, that it arose out of an inability to reject society's pervasive double standard with regard to Negro rights and acceptable means for obtaining those rights.

The answers to one question in the interview shed light on this problem. Respondents were asked whether they felt nonviolence could or should be applied to problems of war and peace. Usually the respondent was pressed to say whether he would be willing to use force in behalf of the United States in the event of war. If those who supported nonviolence in the movement also supported it in case of war, their beliefs may be said to express a general pacifism, however shallow. If, however, we find no such relationship or an inverse relationship, our hypothesis that support for nonviolence in the civil rights movement was an expression of relative conservatism will be strengthened.

The answers to this question fell into three broad groups, as follows:

1. *For conscientious objection to war.* Definite opposition to the use of force in international affairs: "I would be a con-

scientious objector in another war"; "I am for immediate disarmament."

2. *An intermediate position.* The respondent is not sure about being a conscientious objector or supporting disarmament, but he is critical of United States militarism: "I feel the United States should be a lot more careful about getting into war, but I suppose I would have to fight if one started"; "I'm not for unilateral disarmament, but I do feel we've overstressed the military."

3. *Against the position of the conscientious objector.* Force must be used to defend the country: "Nonviolence can't be applied to war—the communists would take us over"; "I would definitely not be a conscientious objector. It's not the same as nonviolence in the movement."

The reaction of the forty-six CORE members* on this question was as follows:

For conscientious objection to national defense	35%
Intermediate position	24
Against the conscientious objection position	22
Don't know, no answer	19

In order to explore polarity of nonviolent positions, let us now combine two dimensions: nonviolence in the movement and conscientious objection to war. For purposes of simplicity we will collapse the two variables into two categories each. On attitudes toward nonviolence in the movement discussed earlier, we combine all those who fell into category 1 (nonviolence as a moral commitment) and category 2 (nonviolence as a technique only). The combined rubric is called "for nonviolence in the movement." We combine category 3 (questioning nonviolence) and category 4 (rejecting nonviolence) as "against or questioning nonviolence in the movement." On the war variable, we will combine categories 1 and 2: those definitely pacifist and those intermediate, calling it "conscientious objection to war"; and we keep category 3: "against the conscientious objection position." We shall omit from this combination those eleven persons who do not have definite positions on both variables. We thus find this relationship between positions on nonviolence in the movement and in national defense:

* Percentages have been rounded out.

CONSCIENTIOUS OBJECTION	*For*	*Against or Questioning*
For	14	10
Against	8	3

The two groups above that represent the consistent violent-nonviolent dimension—those for violence in the movement as well as in national defense and those opposed to violence in both cases—total seventeen persons. The groups representing inconsistent opinions on nonviolence total eighteen: eight persons accept nonviolence for the movement but reject it for national defense and ten persons question nonviolence for the movement but support it in national defense. The positions of these last two types were clearly determined by considerations other than acceptance or rejection of pacifist philosophy. It is suggested, therefore, that the respondents who would not defend themselves against white segregationists but would fight against enemies of the country are ideological moderates who accept the prevalent social value of doubting the Negro's right of self-defense while accepting the popular view that everyone has to defend his country from those defined as enemies. The ten respondents who would consider the use of violence in the movement but reject or question the use of force in national defense represent a radical departure from prevailing values. In line with these assumptions, we might hypothesize that most of the respondents who are consistently nonviolent represent an intermediate position between radicalism and moderation.

The combination of the two questions on nonviolence, in the movement and in national defense, has now given us three "types" relative to the two variables:

	NONVIOLENCE IN THE MOVEMENT	
CONSCIENTIOUS OBJECTION	*For*	*Against or Questioning*
For	Nonviolent Type (intermediate)	Radical Type
Against	Moderate Type	*

* The three respondents who consistently supported the use of violence will be dropped from the remainder of the discussion because their number is too small for us to generalize about.

To test the hypothesis that these three types represent positions running from moderation to radicalism, it would be useful to see how they are related to other dimensions of opinion. During the interviews a count was made of positive and negative attitudes toward all aspects of American society. The comments fell into the following general categories:

NEGATIVE ATTITUDES*

1. *Criticism of the economic system.* "Civil rights can't be attained under capitalism"; "The whole class system has to be changed."

2. *Criticism of the role of the United States abroad.* "The United States spreads racism all over the world"; "They are hypocritical telling other nations about freedom"; "The United States doesn't dare to send outspoken Negroes abroad."

3. *Praise of conventionally defined enemies.* "The Russian system has a lot to say for it"; "Castro got rid of racism, which shows it can be done."

4. *Criticism of the federal government as being lax on civil rights.* "Kennedy doesn't have any real feeling for the Negro"; "They only move when you really push them."

5. *Praise of radicals.* "I can see how Du Bois would go communist"; "I never considered the communists my enemies."

6. *Criticisms of American culture.* "America is overconformist and materialistic"; "Americans are congenitally intolerant of all minorities"; "I've thought of living in Europe to get away from here."

7. *Disparagement of myths and traditions.* "I don't feel I have any country"; "Hitler helped the Negro out by starting the war."

8. *Statements claiming that if the United States doesn't straighten out, the movement will end in black nationalism or violence* (when these are clearly used as warnings against the United States, or with a sense of satisfaction,

---

* This count excludes all those statements that refer only to a local or regional racial situation. Southern respondents frequently deplore the local situation while voicing confidence in the federal government or the nation as a whole. Only criticisms referring clearly to the whole nation or the federal government were counted. Also excluded were those remarks having to do with the violence-nonviolence dimension that were used to construct the first typology. For example, "Violence on the part of Negroes is the only thing that moves our federal government."

not when expressed in connection with serious concern for preventing such an outcome). "If whites don't come around, Negroes will have to fight back"; "I don't know how much longer people are going to take it nonviolently."

9. *Statements that the United States may become fascist or that the military may take over.* "The military would blow the Negroes up if they could"; "We are already so close to fascism that we don't know how things will go."

10. *Reported membership in left-wing groups* (Socialist, Trotskyist, Fair Play for Cuba, Independent Progressive party).

POSITIVE ATTITUDES*

1. *Allusions to the good past performance of the federal government in civil rights.* "Kennedy has done more than any previous President"; "The courts have really supported us."

2. *Expressions of confidence in the future good works of the federal government.* "Kennedy will do more for us after he is reelected"; "I feel sure the government will protect us against violence."

3. *Support for the general framework of American society and government.* "Our laws are good already—it's just a matter of enforcement"; "Civil rights can be attained under the present system."

4. *Support of the United States against conventionally defined enemies.* "We have to make sure that communists don't influence our movement"; "We wouldn't want Khrushchev to run our country."

5. *Identification with American traditions and heroes.* "The movement is heroic to me, like the American Revolution."

A scale was constructed by counting up the negative and positive expressions of opinion in each interview and subtracting one from the other. The scale runs from +2 (a pre-

* One positive point was given if the respondent did not mention the American system during the interview. This was done because respondents were generally not probed on this score. However, remarks about the American system came up spontaneously during the interview and since the overwhelming majority of them were negative, it was felt that no mention by the respondent indicated a positive attitude—at least by comparison with other respondents who did comment.

ponderance of two positive over all negative mentions) to −10 (a preponderance of ten negative over all positive mentions).* The distribution of positive and negative scores among the forty-six respondents is given below:

+2	9%
+1	35
−1 to −2	28
−3 to −6	17
−7 to −10	11

Is there a connection between the typology and the respondent's attitudes toward American society? We find these correlations: †

	+2	+1	−1 to −2	−3 to −6	−7 to −10
Moderate	1	5	1	1	
Nonviolent	1	6	5		2
Radical			3	4	3
Total	2	11	9	5	5

These relationships support the hypothesis that a moderate-radical dimension determined the attitude of many respondents toward the use of nonviolence in the integration movement. All ten persons dubbed radical (those favoring or considering the use of violence in the movement but opposing violence in national defense) expressed predominantly negative attitudes toward the American system, seven of them falling into the two most negative groupings. The eight persons labeled moderate (those favoring nonviolence for the movement but willing to fight for their country) are concentrated on the positive end of the ranking, with only one case falling into one of the two most negative groups.

The fourteen respondents in the nonviolent category were

* This is certainly not an exact scale. Interviewer guidance in this type of loosely structured interview cannot be completely eliminated, nor can the type or intensity of the comment be taken into account. As a rough indicator, however, I am confident that the scale reflects the general attitudes of the various respondents.

† The original sample of forty-six is reduced to thirty-two by the elimination of eleven respondents who did not state a definite position on nonviolence and war and of the three who took the atypical position of favoring violence in the movement and supporting war.

intermediate in their attitudes inasmuch as they generally leaned toward the positive end of the American system scale, although only one was extremely positive. In terms of general rejection of the United States, these people appeared to be liberals who rejected the society to a mild extent. They were not, however, alienated to the point of accepting the idea of violence in the integration struggle. Their support for non-violence in the movement was, at least in large part, an expression of their faith in the American system and their partial acceptance of conventional American views with regard to the Negro's right to fight for equality.

To further illustrate that the categories—radical, non-violent, and moderate—corresponded with progressive degrees of rejection of prevailing American values, we look at the association between these types and one other index of attitudes toward American values. An analysis and a count were made of respondents' attitudes toward America as reflected in their opinions of the black nationalist movement. Such an analysis cannot rest with the assumption that approval of black nationalism automatically means rejection of American values. As E. U. Essien-Udom has pointed out, black nationalism both rejects and accepts American values.[2] In its anti-white racism and its rejection of national unity, as well as in its emphasis on violence and vengeance, black nationalism opposes American values. But in its de facto emphasis on middle class virtues and in its desire to retreat from open struggle against the status quo in favor of building up Negro businesses and pushing individual upward mobility, black nationalism accepts prevailing values. The respondents' attitudes, then, were grouped according to which of these aspects of black nationalism were praised or criticized.

ATTITUDES TOWARD NATIONALISM INDICATING
NEGATIVE FEELINGS TOWARD AMERICA

1. *Reverse racism helps the Negro self-image.* "It helps to hear them deny the usual version of Negro history"; "They are right to stress black virtues and minimize the glories of living with the white man."

2. *Nationalists have an effective appeal to the masses.* "They really speak to the problems of the poor man."

3. *Nationalists are good because they are militant, outspoken.* "They really see the white man for what he is."

4. *Generalized sympathy and understanding of the position.*
"I can sympathize with their radicalism, racism, desire to
separate."

5. *Nationalists are unsatisfactory because they are really conservative.* "An excuse for not getting into action"; "Really
bourgeois"; "Running away from the struggle."

ATTITUDES TOWARD NATIONALISM INDICATING
POSITIVE FEELINGS TOWARD AMERICA

1. *Express antiracist emphasis* (whether made in connection
with the nationalist issue or not). "I don't think a person
is right just because he is black"; "I teach my children not
to think about race at all."

2. *Nationalists are wrong to preach separation, black supremacy, violence, and hate.* "It is just another kind of racism";
"Separation is wrong"; "The Nationalists' emphasis on
violence, hate and vengeance is wrong."

3. *Nationalists are keeping us from attaining absolute equality.* "The nationalists compete with us and frustrate the
goals of our movement."

4. *Distrust of nationalists.* "Nationalists are nasty, hypocritical, aggressive, and not sincere."

Again, a count was made of positive and negative comments and one subtracted from the other. The association
with our moderation-radicalism typology among thirty-two

	+1 or more	0	−1 or less
Moderate	5	3	0
Nonviolent	6	4	4
Radical	1	5	4
Total	12	12	8

respondents emerges, and again we see that the respondents
who fell into the moderate category were those most supportive of the United States against the dissident values of
black nationalism. Radical respondents were those most negative toward the United States, and the nonviolent respondents
were those who held an intermediate position.

Moderate-Radical Typology and Race and Region

It is interesting to note how differently Negro and white CORE members among the thirty-two respondents were distributed among the three political types. Negro respondents

	Negro	White
Moderate	6	1
Nonviolent	8	7
Radical	7	3
Total	21	11

were more polarized in their attitudes than whites. Thirteen of the Negroes were either moderate or radical. Only eight were in the intermediate, nonviolent category. Whites, on the other hand, were predominantly nonviolent (seven), with only four falling into either of the two extremes. What happens to this racial breakdown when region is held constant is indicated in the table, which gives us an explanation of the polarized pattern of Negro attitudes. We see that Southern Negroes

	NEGRO		WHITE	
	Northern Chapters	*Southern Chapters*	*Northern Chapters*	*Southern Chapters*
Moderate	—	6	—	1
Nonviolent	4	4	5	2
Radical	5	2	2	1
Total	9	12	7	4

were predominantly moderates and Northern Negroes predominantly radical. Whites in both regions were generally nonviolent. This finding suggests that although the three types previously seemed to represent three positions on a continuum of alienation from prevailing American values, they also reflected a difference in "style" between whites and Negroes in the movement.

Summary

As stated previously, whites generally came to the movement with fairly stable, well-defined liberal views. They usually came from, and continued to have their roots in, the intellectual liberal-left community. Their participation in the movement, which usually overshadowed other commitments, was one of a range of liberal political activities. They were unlikely to support national self-defense because the advocacy of peace was one of the major tenets of their liberal faith. They were, on the other hand, under no direct, personal, emotional pressure with regard to the race question and so were unlikely to experience that extreme alienation from American society represented by violence—even self-defensive violence—in the integration movement. Negroes, however, required no elaborate liberal conditioning to bring them into the movement. The movement was their cause. And although only small segments of the Negro community became activists, they did not need exceptional political sophistication or markedly critical views vis-à-vis other aspects of American society. Negroes were always under direct emotional pressure resulting from segregation and discrimination. Therefore, the potential for great radicalism was present in their personal relationship to the issue. In the next chapter a closer examination of Negroes in these three categories is made in order to see under what conditions the radical stand developed and to see if, for Negroes, the nonviolent position represented an unstable, transitional phase from moderation to radicalism.

NOTES

1. For an imaginative discussion of social movements as collective solutions to individual problems, see Hans Toch, *The Social Psychology of Social Movements* (Indianapolis: Bobbs-Merrill, 1965).
2. E. U. Essien-Udom, *Black Nationalism: A Search for Identity in America* (Chicago: University of Chicago Press, 1962), pp. 325–339.

CHAPTER 8

Southern Moderates
and Northern Radicals

In his *Anatomy of a Revolution,* Crane Brinton describes the typical revolutionary group as one whose status is rising along certain dimensions at the same time that its claims to other, parallel types of status are being frustrated.[1] The typical revolutionary group has been experiencing rising economic status while being denied commensurate political power and/ or social recognition. As the status of such a group rises along one or more dimensions, its expectation of greater overall status greatly exceeds its actual advance, thus giving rise to a steadily increasing sense of relative deprivation.* At the same time, the fact that the group does have a certain amount of economic, educational, or other advantages gives it the self-confidence and practical means with which to attack the established order.

Upward Mobility, Status Discrepancy, and Radicalism

Sociologists have pointed to a phenomenon on the individual level parallel to Brinton's analysis of the group. An individual who combines several statuses that are inconsistent —for example, high income and low ethnic status—is more likely to question the social order than a person whose statuses are consistent or "crystallized." Persons with low status crystallization are said to suffer from "status discrepancy." The sociologist Gerhard Lenski showed that at all status levels high status discrepancy is associated with the favoring of such liberal measures as government health insurance, price controls, and extension of government powers. His explanation is that persons with poorly crystallized statuses are exposed to greater rebuff and unpleasantness, generally from persons

* The term "relative deprivation" refers to the gap between what an individual expects and what he actually receives. It expresses the idea that the deprivation or frustration a person experiences depends not simply on his circumstances but also on the relationship between circumstances and expectations.

of higher status. This stimulates a desire to attack the higher status levels and turns easily toward left-wing criticism of the whole social order. He claims that persons with discrepant statuses tend to withdraw from contact with those of solidly high status, thus confirming his theory that they suffer from rebuff.[2]

Particularly relevant for our purposes is Lenski's finding that although all patterns of status inconsistency show a positive association with liberalism, low ethnic status combined with education and high income show the closest association. Also relevant to our case is Erving Goffman's finding that status discrepancy produces the greatest desire for change in the highest stratum, the reason being that people at high occupational levels find it most difficult to separate social contacts from business contacts and are thus unable to protect themselves against strain by the usual method of dividing their separate status dimensions into separate social roles.[3]

This body of theory sheds considerable light on the question of why certain Negroes in the direct action movement developed radical ideology while others maintained a more moderate ideological position. As radical, nonviolent, and moderate Negroes are compared on various characteristics, it is interesting to note that one dimension underlies all the comparisons: the radical Negroes had previously adopted more of the cultural and social traits of white middle class society than had the moderates, the nonviolent types holding an intermediate position. The Negro who was socially and culturally most like the white man—moving most easily in white society and competing most successfully with whites—was also most critical of American society and most militant in his attitude toward the movement.

If a parallel is drawn between the assimilation of Negroes and the assimilation of European immigrants into American society, we can look upon the Southern Negro sharecropper or tenant farmer as the "foreigner." His children who migrate to Northern or Southern cities and take up service trades and unskilled jobs constitute the first-generation "immigrants." The next two generations, those who get to college and try to move into white-collar and professional jobs, generally in Northern cities, constitute the upwardly mobile segment of the "second and third generation."

It is in the experience of these second- and third-generation upwardly mobile Negro Americans that an essential difference between the fate of Negroes and of other immigrants is found. Whereas the second- and third-generation European immigrants were able to shed their foreign identities and gain acceptance along all major status dimensions, their opposite numbers in the Negro group moved into frustrating situations of acute status discrepancy: having high education but limited access to high-status jobs or, having achieved high-status jobs, continuing to suffer from social ostracism. Whereas the various immigrant groups were able to gain entrance into the American middle class through a combination of group political effort and individual mobility, upwardly mobile Negroes found that even after several generations of upward striving and acculturation, their problem could not be solved. This fact, more than the comparative failure of the mass of Negroes to attain any sort of upward mobility, produced the radicalism of CORE and similar direct action groups during the early 1960s.

The data on the social background of Negro CORE members showed that they were drawn largely from this upwardly mobile vanguard, which had run head on into the barriers to further mobility and full acceptance. Indeed, within CORE itself, it was those individuals who had moved furthest out of the Negro subculture into the white middle class—those with the highest status—who were most radical.

A word of caution is in order here. To say that the most politically militant people came from this group is not to say that middle class Negroes in general were radical. The bulk of the black bourgeoisie still is, as Franklin Frazier has pointed out, apolitical and overconformist.[4] Militancy is an alternative reaction characteristic of only a small minority. The point here is that it was *only* from within the ranks of relatively acculturated Negroes that ideological radicals emerged during the 1960–1963 period.

Regional Environment and Radicalism

The most striking fact about our respondents is the association between their ideological position and the region in which they lived:

	South	North	Total
Moderate	7	0	7
Nonviolent	3	4	7
Radical	2	5	7

All seven moderates were members of Southern chapters and all seven were born and brought up in the South. By contrast, five of the seven radicals were from Northern chapters and two of the five had been raised in the North.* Both of the Southern radicals had visited outside the South; only one of the Southern moderates had had this experience. The non-violent types fall between.

With regard to race, the gap between official policy and social reality is infinitely greater in the North than in the South even though official philosophy and popular belief both have it that the North is the land of equal opportunity. The phrase "regardless of race, color, or creed" is stamped on every major Northern institution but is widely ignored in actual practice. The North raises the highest possible expectations of equality among Negroes and then fails to deliver on this promise. This gap is particularly evident among Northern Negroes from middle class homes; they are frequently shielded from the worst realities of discrimination during their formative years and consequently enter upon adult life with a very high level of expectation. Southern barriers to mobility, although objectively much greater, create less sense of deprivation and frustration because they are "out in the open" and officially recognized. These barriers are taken into account from the beginning. This factor is well illustrated in the following account by a Southern respondent who came North after finishing college in order to take advantage of greater employment opportunities:

In the South, there was the feeling that nothing could be done. There were some jobs you knew you couldn't apply for; you'd just get kicked out of the office—no hopes there while the attitude is this way. I will admit that I hated the implications of the thing at the time but there was nothing you could do about it. We felt you could go North to improve things. That was my own reason, that I thought employment opportunity here would be held in fair play—in which I was deceived and this was a main reason for joining the civil rights group. I was out here one summer while I was still in school, looking around. At that time they all said they couldn't do anything for me because I didn't have my degree, but when I came out here after finishing school the story had changed. I went to a private employment agency and was told to come back—and I would come back. I always did dress properly . . . and I was shaved and combed and neat. And I saw white

* Only three Negroes in the entire sample were born in the North.

men who came in there with their collars open, seen them sent out to jobs that were advertised for management trainees—I've even seen the people there send those guys home for a tie—but they would tell me to come back all the time. And another agency, they took me in the back room and sort of patted me on the shoulder and said they didn't care if I was green or gray or black but the companies keep them in business, so they couldn't go against their wishes. I felt worse about this discrimination than about what was so obvious in the South—open segregation in employment—because there you knew for a fact it exists.

In terms of the concept of relative deprivation, this respondent upon coming North clearly shifted his reference group from Negroes to whites, thus increasing his level of expectation far in excess of the actual increase in employment opportunity.

One other difference between the two regions must be taken into account here. It may be safe to assume that, given the same initial psychological makeup, an increase in repression and frustration for a group will increase its expressed hostility toward society. However, there is ample evidence that persons *raised* under repressive conditions may develop a psychological incapacity to express hostility or even to consciously experience it.

Bertram Karon has gathered evidence to show that the Southern environment tends to develop a Negro personality that is well equipped to "swallow" frustration and ill equipped to fight it openly—regardless of method: individual rebellion, political action, direct aggression, or ideological rebellion. As a result of giving several groups of Southern and Northern Negroes, as well as Northern whites, projective examinations designed to test ability to deal with aggression, Karon concluded that Southern Negroes have a greater tendency than Northern Negroes to "deny" aggressive situations; that is, they fail to perceive aggression when it occurs and have less capacity to express counteraggression on any level. The Northern Negro personality resembled the Northern white personality quite closely on these characteristics, thus differing sharply from the passivity characteristic of the Southern Negro.[5]

The two Negro Southern radicals in our sample had backgrounds and personalities strikingly different from those of most Southern Negroes in that both were extremely light-skinned, one being light enough to "pass" easily. Skin color has long been a high status characteristic among Negroes and whites. The lighter of the two respondents had always enjoyed fooling whites by passing for white and entering places that excluded Negroes. Once, while traveling on a train, he became obviously friendly with a white girl and spent the day sitting with his arm around her and winking at Negro employees who spotted him as Negro and enjoyed sharing the joke with him. The other respondent said that he and his family knew themselves to be closely related to the leading former slave-owning white family in his home town:

> My great-grandfather was a white plantation owner. Grandfather used to tell me how his father deserted his mother. My grandfather was a carpenter—he founded a town in Louisiana which is named after him . . . Miscegenation brought about changes all over the world. Pinchback in Louisiana was a mulatto; Beethoven and Dodds in France were mulattoes.

These two radical Southerners also had exceptionally high status fathers. One was an independent contractor and the son had become a partner in the family business. The other father was a skilled worker, and the son was a student planning to become a psychiatrist. All but one of the *other* Southern respondents were children of unskilled workers or of farmers.

High Status and Radicalism

The child first forms views of his own status by learning to recognize the status accorded his family in the community. Parental status is especially important in our sample because many of the respondents were students who had not yet attained firm statuses of their own. The table below shows the relationship between the father's status and the CORE respondent's ideological type.

	Farmer, Unskilled, Semiskilled	Skilled, White-Collar, Proprietor, Professional	Total
Moderate	5	2	7
Nonviolent	4	3	7
Radical	1	6	7

As expected, moderate types came predominantly from low-status families; radicals were again at the opposite extreme; and nonviolent types were intermediate. The same pattern is repeated with regard to the fathers' education. Fathers of moderates had 7.3 mean years of education; fathers of non-violent types had 9.6; and fathers of radicals had 10.3.

The way the fathers' status influenced the self-confidence of the children was illustrated in the contrasting recollections of two respondents, both born and raised in the South. One, the son of a doctor, said:

> Where I came from in Arkansas, well, the whole state was so terribly poor, doctors were very rare—both Negro and white. My father had a unique position as a doctor. I mean at that time you could say to a white man, "You son of a bitch," because you were educated. They had a convention of Yale graduates once in Arkansas and there were two Negroes and three whites—in the whole state—I know because my brother went there to speak and told me about it.

The other, the daughter of a tenant farmer, reported:

> Since I was a child I was never happy with the situation. I grew up on a farm in Georgia. My daddy had a big farm. And he had to go to the white man to get credit to buy the food and the fertilizer—and always being told you're in second place. I think you have to be unhappy with that situation before you can be the kind of person who'll join CORE. I was always unhappy with it. On the farm you had to be a good nigger. I came to the city to get away from that and of course I found that same problem here. You carry it with you wherever you go.

The doctor's son qualified as a radical in the typology; the other respondent was a moderate.

It may be assumed that the current extent of the individual's education influenced his self-image and self-confidence. A doctoral candidate would have higher expectations of equal treatment than a college sophomore, even if the sophomore expected to go on to a doctoral degree. The data on mean years of schooling completed again shows the association between high status and radicalism. Moderates had completed 12.4 years of school; nonviolent types had completed 12.8; and radicals showed the astonishingly high mean of 16.3 years completed.

"Aggravation" and Radicalism

The typical lower-status Southern respondent lived in comparative isolation from whites. He had few actual contacts with them, and those he had were characterized by social distance, maintained through impersonality or superiority and subordination. On the other hand, the Northern middle class Negro came in constant contact with whites. These contacts were often highly ambiguous, that is, there was no clear structuring in terms of separation or subordination. In fact, some of them were of quite intimate nature. The acculturated Negro, in short, "rubbed up" against whites daily, frequently in a deeply personal manner. He had to constantly test his white associates to discover the degree of their prejudice. He often had to "take chances" on whites and he was frequently disappointed. For example, on the job or at school he might have congenial personal relations with white associates, joining them for lunch and coffee breaks, and then find himself excluded from dinners and parties shared by the others in the group. Or, he might attend parties and socialize with white women who would chat with him or dance with him, but who would refuse to date him. He might have been fairly good friends with a boss who had decided that it would be unwise to promote him. He might even, as in the case of one radical respondent, have married a white woman who was later unable to adjust to the difficulties of an interracial marriage.

These experiences—because they were daily and inescapable and because they reached into the individual's deepest feelings and most intimate relationships—created a peculiar type of bitterness and frustration. We shall call this phenomenon "aggravation," to signify its similarity to physical rubbing or chafing, which may create withdrawal, calluses, or inflammations, depending on the individual reaction.

This factor was illustrated in exaggerated form in the case of one individual whom we were able to "follow" from a Southern to a Northern environment. "O" was first interviewed during the summer of 1962. At that time he was nineteen years old and was working as a voter registration fieldworker in his home state of Mississippi. He held an ideological position that was midway between moderate and nonviolent. He felt that he would serve if drafted, but he hoped to get into the medical corps, where he would not have to fight, because he considered himself by nature and philosophy nonviolent. In response to a question on the Black Muslims he said:

> I can't go along with that, because I think everyone is the result of their environment—the white people are brought up that

way and don't know any better—and I don't believe in hate, like that . . . I can admire a segregationist if he believes it is right, but the ones that do it just to keep a position, well, I guess I have to look on him with sorrow and pity.

Despite numerous experiences with arrest and violence, the respondent expressed no hostility toward whites. He was prepared to accept considerable subjugation without bitterness. For example, during the interview he asked the interviewer, without any sign of rancor, but merely with a trace of curiosity and disbelief:

Inge, when you're in the South—tell me the truth—don't you sometimes feel superior? I mean you see all the Negroes so poor and uneducated and there are so many places you can go that they can't go . . .

With regard to his work in the movement, he said:

There is a slight possibility of getting beaten up here, but even if I get killed—well, it's foolish to talk about getting killed—but if I did, well, I'd at least have known why I was doing it . . . If I can help a few people, well then, I know there will be thousands more to take my place.

A year later O was brought to a Northern city through the good offices of white friends in the movement. He moved into a house with white CORE members and entered college. The interviewer had the opportunity of becoming reacquainted with him during his first six months of residence in the North. After a few months, he had become extremely radical and bitter on the subject of race. Of his personal experience, he told the interviewer:

I am so completely discouraged about getting a part-time job. I feel as if no matter how hard I try there will be discrimination against me. I apply at all these places, but I'm almost sure none of them will hire me. I get so sick of trying because you never know whether you're not just wasting your time . . . I know this is foolish but whenever I go into the library at college and have to sit down at a table with a white guy I feel as though he might be hating me—not wanting me to sit there, you know. I don't know whether that's true or not but I just always suspect it. For the last few months I've had the same nightmare all the time. I dream I'm walking to school and I get about halfway there and this young white kid drives up in a car and runs me over—I can see his face and I know he hates me.

During these few months, O had done a complete about-face ideologically. He was reading Robert Williams and *Muhammad Speaks* and was seriously questioning the movement's commitment to nonviolence. His attitude toward America had become extremely negative and he declared himself unwilling to serve in the army not because he disliked killing but because, as he put it, "This isn't my country."

His experience with aggravation was worsened by his peculiar sensitivity and his fear of contact with whites, the result of his change from a Southern to a Northern environment.

This reaction by O also holds for Northern middle class Negroes. Those raised in the North start out more confident and less fearful of contacts, but this advantage is counteracted by the fact that they have much higher expectations and are in just as much danger of disappointment. The following accounts of Northern-raised Negroes illustrate the factor of aggravation in their lives:

There is a certain type of white man who will always pull something on you. Like a guy I used to work for at the school—and he would always slap me on the back and let me know every way he could that he didn't feel superior and we were just buddy-buddy. Well, one day he wanted me to help him build some steps there and he didn't know how to go about measuring and planning the thing at all, and so he said, "Oh, you do it for me." And I said, "No, you do it, that isn't my job. I'm not getting paid for doing that." And then he just commanded me, "You do it or else"—you see, that's how they really feel and it always comes out in the end.

In choosing friends, it isn't enough just for them to be for integration or the general ideal. It means more if I can trust a person in interpersonal relations. It's a question of faith in the person and whether I can overcome a fear of damage to myself, like a person who would not be OK. If somebody is in a hospital and doesn't notice all the nurses are white and nurses aides are Negroes, then it's because they accept the social definition. This doesn't mean they support discrimination. On the other hand, I'll probably tend to be unfair, I'll tend to shove him into a tough category initially until he proves otherwise. If you only think about the problem when you see me, that irritates me right there. I can only say that if you look at the world and see the structure of occupations and distribution of Negroes and don't feel it's discrimination then you must have some other explanation for the stratification and well . . .

Exposure to Radical Ideas

Relative deprivation and aggravation result in frustration, anger, and other emotional reactions. But such feelings are not automatically translated into political radicalism, even by persons participating in the movement. There also must be access to such radical ideas as an analysis of society that would justify a negative attitude toward "America" and that would legitimate the idea of great militancy with regard to the movement. And in discussing contact with radical ideas, we must also take into account the opposite contact, with groups that foster conservatism. Most of the Negroes in our sample claimed membership in a church, with the overwhelming majority belonging to Methodist and Baptist denominations. These traditional Negro churches—although they sometimes participated in the movement, particularly in the Christian Leadership Conferences of Martin Luther King—were still a conservative influence in relation to the CORE groups. All the churches favored nonviolence for the movement. Indeed, the Negro Christian viewpoint was a cornerstone of nonviolent adherence. While most Negroes in our sample claimed nominal membership, there was wide variation in church attendance. If we posit that those who attended church one or more times a month—the usual attendance being four times monthly—were more influenced by church conservatism than those who did not attend, we should expect that non-attenders were more radical than attenders, and the table below bears out this expectation.

	Some Church Attendance	Never Attend Church
Moderate	7	0
Nonviolent	6	1
Radical	1	6

Most of our respondents had belonged to the NAACP and other less radical integration groups prior to joining CORE. None of the moderates had ever participated in any group to the left of the NAACP. Among the nonviolents, two had belonged to Democratic party groups, and although these are moderate in comparison with CORE, they may indicate some political stimulation and some contact with radical ideas. One other nonviolent respondent had previously belonged to the

Student Nonviolent Coordinating Committee, a group similar to and at that time only slightly more militant than CORE.

The picture was very different among the radical respondents. Five of the seven radicals had belonged to groups of similar or greater radicalism than CORE, such as the Independent Progressive party, Socialist party, Turn Toward Peace, Southern Educational Fund, Young People's Socialist League, Jack London Club (Marxist), and the Du Bois Society. All these respondents had absorbed Marxist, pacifist, and other radical ideologies to varying degrees. Table 6 summarizes the various characteristics associated with radicalism.

TABLE 6   **Summary of Characteristics Associated with Ideological Types**

	REGION		FATHER'S OCCUPATION		Father's Mean Education (in years)	Respondent's Mean Education	No. with Previous Membership in Radical Organizations
	North	South	Blue Collar	White Collar			
Moderate	0	7	5	2	7.3	12.4	0
Nonviolent	4	3	3	4	9.6	12.8	1
Radical	5	2	1	6	10.3	16.3	5

Two Case Histories

For a more intimate picture of how the characteristics discussed above interacted to produce radicals and moderates, we give the case histories of two respondents: a "typical" Northern radical and a "typical" Southern moderate.

GEORGE: A RADICAL NORTHERN NEGRO

George was an exceptionally handsome young man of twenty-five whose cynicism was softened by a personally warm, charming manner. He was obviously very bright, though given to short lapses of attention, during which he seemed to withdraw suddenly and completely. He described his family as "middle class and light-skinned, the typical 'black bourgeois' pictured in Frazier's book." The family laid great stress on their light complexion and objected to his dating girls much darker than himself. "Looking back on our attitudes," said

George, "I'd say we were trying very hard to be white though not admitting it."

Born and raised in a large Northern city, he attended a predominantly white high school and college and was fairly well accepted by his white associates on the basis of "not being like those other Negroes." He described the typical whites with whom he came in contact during these years as

> people who say things like "Some of my best friends are Negroes" and talk about how terrible the South is—and then they tell me how I'm different from all those other Negroes. The more liberal part of them will say, "Of course we wouldn't mind having a Negro neighbor—but he should be chosen very carefully." They mean they wouldn't mind living next to Ralph Bunche. The conservative type would mind, but only because of the threat to property values.

After earning his master's degree, George spent a year in Europe. There he realized just how dissatisfied and uncomfortable he had always felt at home and he thought seriously of becoming an expatriate, thus escaping the race problem forever. Instead, he returned to the United States and enrolled as a graduate student in a large Northern university, where he met two white acquaintances from his old college and became friendly with them. These two friends had become quite radical and were members of a Marxist study group, CORE, and SNCC. Through them, George was first exposed to political ideas and activities. Up to this time he had been apolitical.

> It's hard for me to reconstruct my previous feelings now. Of course, I had opinions on civil rights—I was in favor of it. But I had no idea of doing something, not even with the NAACP. Joining anything was kind of repugnant to me—like it was a public admission that I was a Negro. After I got into this political circle here through H and J I began to make a conscious effort to get out of this standard black-bourgeois feeling that if I don't do anything about civil rights and don't join anything, maybe nobody will think I'm a Negro—you know, like maybe they'll think I'm white—so I'll just dissociate myself from the people in the ghetto.

Eventually George joined CORE and SNCC and continued his close association with members of the Marxist study group. It is important to note that these associations increased the respondent's ability and willingness to formulate radical opinions and also functioned to decrease his general sense of alienation from the country and his frustrations about his own identity. He reported:

About the time I joined CORE the idea of being a Negro began to be more acceptable to me. It's hard to say which came first, the involvement in politics or the change in feeling. I suppose I got involved partly because I wanted to change my feelings.

Heretofore, he had never felt completely comfortable in his relationship with whites. His attitude toward the white world was deeply ambivalent. He admired it and wished to emulate it; by virtue of his education and social position he saw himself inevitably immersed in it. Yet he felt an underlying bitterness because of the impossibility of finding in it genuine acceptance of his total identity—including his inescapable identity as a Negro. Now he discovered whites who met him on an entirely different level:

When I first picketed with CORE it gave me the feeling that I could do something, and also that I was being a Negro and acting like it—not being ashamed of it. At the same time I felt I was being part of a movement of doing things that were strongly approved of by people whose opinion was important to me. I felt that I could do this with the group and simultaneously feel accepted, and like my acceptance was not based on the fact that "you're different, you're not the same as all those other Negroes." I didn't have to be somebody's "best friend," the exception everybody approved of—which meant being white, really . . . Looking back I realize that I was in this position with my white friends at school and college all the time. I was always winning approval and respect from them based on how little Negro I was. The people I met here—they were committed to civil rights struggle—it was evident that it was possible to identify with the Negroes in the slums and in the South and still feel that I hadn't lost the respect of those people.

Having found whites who were solidly on his side relieved his ambivalence and frustration and increased and clarified his dislike of and opposition toward the "wishy-washy liberals" with whom he had previously been in contact. Of them, he said:

They refuse to get committed. They believe in having an open mind—which means a vacant mind—they talk about extremists of the left. They are for integration but opposed to the "haste that creates deep scars."

Through participation in the movement, ambivalence and alienation had been transformed into a feeling of involvement and a clear demand for rapid change "or else."

> When I went to Europe I thought in terms of running away from the whole problem—moving to another country. But since I joined CORE, that's one thing it has done for me: I feel much more like I am part of the country and I feel more like staying here and working on the issue. I find some of my identity in being part of the movement. It's an identity with the masses and with myself as a Negro and having some reason to be proud of that fact. It's the general atmosphere of people being committed to revolution—like the American Revolution —it has heroic overtones of manly virtues and bravery.

Being now part of the nation, he was prepared to berate it strongly for its shortcomings. He saw American society as "in fact an Anglo-Saxon culture and not this fictitious melting pot people talk about." American society has always demanded complete conformity as the price of admission. Of the Negro it demanded that he become as white as possible. Before the race problem can be solved, the respondent felt, there will have to be economic planning, public works programs, and much greater commitment to welfare. A basic minimum standard of living and the right to work will have to be guaranteed to everyone. From an economic and political viewpoint, there is more wrong with the country than just segregation. The country will have to spend more on its citizens and less on war, missiles, and space racing. To accomplish this, George saw the need for drastic political realignment.

> Any solutions to the problem would now be politically unrealizable with the present power distribution—not to be Marxist about it, but I think power will have to be shifted to the working class and to Negroes, to the people being hurt by the situation.

The respondent's position vis-à-vis the Black Muslims was complex and revealing. He berated them for being really bourgeois: "Their greatest wish is for a chain of Howard Johnsons from coast to coast—only all black." He felt that black nationalism gave many Negroes he knew an excuse for doing nothing concrete although they talked a lot about how radical they were. On the other hand, he found obvious satisfaction in the militancy and outspokenness of the Muslims even though he was unable to accept their unqualified racism.

> It is a relief to hear the Muslims speak out. Like when they say, "I'm going to look the white man in the eye and call him a liar every time he opens his mouth." All of which is true— everything they say about whites except for their racist insistence that all whites are inherently evil.

With regard to nonviolence, he said:

> I'm not interested in it. I suppose it is generally the best tactic because 90 percent of the country is white. But to me nonviolence isn't a panacea. I don't know whether it can work in the Deep South, where the forces of law are lawbreakers themselves. There I think you have to have a right of self-defense.

Although he admitted to a natural middle class abhorrence of becoming involved in violence personally, the respondent freely expressed vicarious satisfaction with Negro violence elsewhere:

> Maybe it's pointless, but there was a feeling of release when that Muslim in Mississippi killed the gas station owner. This has a real appeal that, dammit, we're going to pay it back. I remember the description of the scene, how the guy turned a hose on him and he calmly went to his car and got out a gun and very calmly shot the guy—just emptied the gun into him and the guy dragged himself into the gas station and the Negro went back to the car and reloaded the gun and emptied it into the guy again and then drove away.
> . . . I tie up racial pride with things like rebellions in Angola and thinking about raising money for the invasion of South Africa—I wish the United States government would train African troops for the invasion of the South, the way some Southern newspapers claim.

SARAH: A MODERATE SOUTHERN NEGRO

Our moderate respondent was a twenty-seven-year-old widow with four young children. Her husband, a small retailer, had left her a little money, on which she had been supporting her family. Her health was very poor and she required much medical attention, thus making it impossible for her to earn an income of her own. Sarah had been raised on a farm by her grandparents, neither of whom had more than a third-grade education. She herself finished high school. Their greatest claim to status was that the grandmother was a licensed midwife.

The respondent moved in a solidly Negro world. She had no white friends and had only a passing familiarity with whites at CORE conventions. Few whites belonged to her local CORE chapter; she knew none of them well and seemed uninterested in and unconcerned about them.

Sarah thoroughly approved of nonviolence as a tactic for the movement. Significantly enough, she misunderstood the question "Will there be violence on the part of integrationists in future years?" to mean "Will there be more violence against integrationists?" When I clarified that I meant violence from CORE members, she said, "No, never!" This inability to imagine any other tactic stemmed partly from the self-evident validity that the nonviolent course of action had for her; but, even more, from the general inability to speculate beyond present realities that is typical of persons of limited education who have never been exposed to such intellectual exercises.

In recounting her direct action experiences, Sarah gave vent to a good deal of undisguised hostility. But nonviolence seemed to be an adequate vehicle for its expression because her conception of nonviolence was naïve enough to keep her from seeing any contradictions between her hostility and the tactic, and because her hostility was of a type most easily expressed through "passivity with a slight bite." Of nonviolence she said:

> I think you can't fight it. If you don't hit back and you don't talk back, well then, they're just gonna stand around looking stupid—they can't do nothin'. One time we had some hoodlums come up ready to attack us. Well, we didn't say anything —we just referred them to our spokesman. Well, that was really a ghastly lookin' thing. They was just standin' around not knowing what to do.

She remembered some direct action victories with rather vengeful satisfaction:

> When we opened the theaters we worked on it a long time. There was this ticket lady there—she said she'd rather die than sell us tickets. So one night she had to sell us nine tickets and you should have seen her face. I got the biggest kick out of seeing her red face. She told me earlier I could have gotten in by myself if I wasn't with those other people [Author's comment: She is quite light-skinned], and I said we were together and we were all going in together—and in the end we did and she had to sell us the tickets.

Although this respondent was optimistic about the movement's chances of attaining most of its goals, she felt that whites and Negroes would probably never socialize or intermarry and she accepted this as natural:

> I think they [whites and Negroes] will put on an act. They aren't really going to accept each other, just like the Jews and Italians—they get mad if their children want to marry somebody different.

Sarah had high hopes that the movement would open better job opportunities for herself and her children. Indeed, worry about her children's future was one of her main reasons for participating in CORE, even though her level of aspiration for both herself and her children was relatively modest. And she certainly did not feel presently deprived because of overqualification regarding job possibilities in the near future:

> There's great improvement to be had in the employment field and I know that it's gonna affect my children. If they don't all get to college, well, they could come out of high school and get a job typing any place—like white girls—a clean job, like sales lady. I wouldn't mind my daughter being a sales lady. That's not a bad job and you can work up in it—even if she hadn't been to college, she could work up to be a buyer . . . CORE's been talking about getting the phone company as next phase. I'm very interested in that because I'd like to get a job as an operator myself. I'm a physical wreck and I've got to get a sitting-down job. They have on-the-job training with pay. It's a good deal.

With respect to the overall problem of integration, she thought Negroes would have to take more steps into the middle class world before they could be wholly accepted. She predicted that integration would help Negroes become more "cultured." Among other things, it would improve Negro speech: "They'll be exposed to better speech and it'll rub off—won't be so many 'ain'ts' and 'cain'ts,' like what rubbed off on us." She is willing to allow for the fact that whites will need time to "get used to seeing colored kids in the schools, and seeing us around everywhere." Although she did not resent the need for such adjustments, neither was she willing to tarry while they were made. She was determined to enroll her own children in white schools as quickly as possible.

During the interview Sarah made no critical remarks about

American culture, the federal government, the economic system, or white culture. Probing failed to elicit from her any desire for social changes other than those having to do strictly with the race problem. On the subject of pacifism, her views may be described as "ordinary patriotic":

> Pacifism doesn't make sense to me. I mean, you could never fight a war that way. There's too much territory involved. And I mean the communists, they say they're against violence, but they really use it. It's not even common sense. I mean if a war started, they're going to start by dropping a bomb—so what's that except violence?

NOTES

1. Crane Brinton, *The Anatomy of Revolution* (New York: Vintage Books, 1952).
2. Gerhard E. Lenski, "Status Crystallization," *American Sociological Review*, XIX (August, 1954), 405–413; and "Social Participation and Status Crystallization," *American Sociological Review*, XXI (August, 1956), 458–464.
3. Erving Goffman, "Status Consistency and Preference for Change in Power Distribution," *American Sociological Review*, XXII (June, 1957), 275–281.
4. Franklin Frazier, *Black Bourgeoisie* (New York: Free Press, 1957).
5. Bertram P. Karon, *The Negro Personality* (New York: Springer, 1958).

CHAPTER 9

Walking in Other Shoes

"There are a lot of white liberals who sympathize with CORE but who would never join in direct action. Why do you think that you, in particular, took this step?" The answers to this question provide some clues to the difference between white CORE members and those of similar background who remain on the sidelines cheering them on.*

Whites' Involvement in the Direct Action Movement

In answer to the question "Why you?" eleven of the eighteen white respondents described the experience of getting to know a Negro personally, thus learning of the difficulties that Negroes suffer in American society. Four of these experiences were in the context of church groups or educational institutions expressly designed to bring Negroes and whites together. The other experiences took place in neighborhoods, schools, colleges, and work situations that "happened" to be integrated. In only three of these cases had the respondent consciously chosen an interracial milieu.

A striking characteristic of the encounters between our respondents and their Negro friends was that, in nearly every case, the Negro was described as outspoken and bitter about racial injustices, and in several cases this hostility was directed at the white friend. Two respondents described the impression made on them by these encounters:

At college I got to know a Negro man who was an art teacher there, and one day my wife and I went over for coffee and he told us experiences—just facts and events—about what it was like when he left Dallas for the first time to work on a farm. He just described the events in riding buses across the South, and how he tried four times to get in the front entrance of the bus —after this had been permissible in one state—and had the door slammed in his face. All these arbitrary rules from one

* Because we had no control group of non-CORE whites, we can only speculate on the answers to this question.

place to another. I realized that though I used to think I understood Negroes, this was the first time I was really getting inside their experience.

One person affected me most. This was a girl I worked with—the most bitter person I've ever known. We were doing secretarial work together and she was a good friend. She was against CORE because she was against nonviolence. But she had no alternative. She was too angry to take part in it. But she didn't direct it at me—except sometimes when she seemed to lash against everything.

By sharing in the social life of their Negro acquaintances, these respondents were directly exposed to conditions that Negroes confront. One girl reported:

When I worked at the [Northern city] hospital, I became friends with a Negro nurse. My most personal feeling of involvement in the problem came when I wanted to go places with my Negro friend and there were some places she said we didn't go—I guess they knew they would be treated rudely—places they found uncongenial. And then I saw the tremendous housing problem of all the Negroes.

Such encounters were obviously rare in a Southern setting. Only one of the Southern-raised respondents reported having had a close Negro friend in his youth, but the friendship did not include problems of race or politics, nor did he attribute to this relationship any important influences on his ideological development. One atypical case was that of a Northern-born woman who after moving to a Southern city was enlightened on the racial situation by a Negro servant. The exceptional outspokenness in this case may have been due to the servant's realization of the employer's Northern origin and liberal sympathies. In general, the inescapable paternalism that characterizes Negro-white contacts in the South did not lend itself to the type of experience that shaped most of our Northern-raised white CORE members.

Why did the respondents react positively to these confrontations? One reason was that most respondents had been preconditioned to react favorably by liberal family backgrounds. Another reason was that some of the contacts took place in institutional settings where the official policy was favorable to sympathetic Negro-white contact. Two respondents, for example, reported that they attended integrated parochial schools in which the teachers and students took great pride in being integrated. A similar official attitude was reported for the integrated church groups involved.

The prominent role played by these personal contacts in developing the respondent's commitment to civil rights may help explain why militancy is a strongly generational phenomenon among whites. Only in recent years have interracial settings, which provide opportunity for personal contact, become common. And only recently have sufficient numbers of Negroes become outspoken about their problems with whites.

Although personal contact with Negroes was the most frequently mentioned factor in the respondents' own versions of their development, there were only two cases in which it seemed to have been the only or most decisive experience. A number of other factors were mentioned in varying combinations. Nine respondents mentioned their parents' liberal attitudes as important in shaping their own thinking.* Six mentioned the influence of religious training: two involved liberal Protestant denominations; two involved racially liberal attitudes of Catholic parochial schools; one was described as "the influence of the general concern of Judaism with social justice";† and one respondent reported that his Southern Baptist training, though certainly not racially liberal, created in him a desire to be polite and humane to all people and was thereby responsible for an early dislike of open rudeness toward Negroes. Four respondents reported that the influence of a militant white friend or spouse was important in rousing them to a position of militancy and in bringing about their in-

* As indicated in Chapter 4, this is probably the single most important factor in most cases of white militancy. For many it appears to be a "necessary but not sufficient" condition. We do not expand on it further because we are concerned with some of the more "sufficient" conditions.
† Because a large proportion of our white CORE members were ethnically Jewish, it may be of interest to quote this respondent's account of the influence of Judaism on his thinking. Here may be revealed, in exceptionally explicit terms, some of the subtle influences which account for the high Jewish participation in CORE. "If you want to understand the moral sense that comes out of Judaism, you should read the Haggada service for Passover. It's all there very explicitly in the ritual. It talks about the Jews being freed from slavery in Egypt and that they have an obligation because they have been freed . . . You naturally derive from it a sense of identity with the persons who were slaves and a feeling of obligation to follow it up because God had set you free." Possibly the longstanding Jewish experience with persecution and alienation—sometimes leading to political radicalism—is a factor of even greater importance.

volvement in civil rights activities. Three attributed part of their development to a liberal college atmosphere, and four reported that other political commitments led to their involvement in nonviolent direct action for civil rights. All of the respondents mentioned several of the foregoing factors as interacting in their development. Probably no single factor among those mentioned could, by itself, bring a person to the point of direct action.

Negroes as the Major Reference Group

The same factors that were instrumental in pushing our respondents toward a militant civil rights commitment—intimate personal contact and Negro outspokenness—were greatly intensified within CORE. They created an orientation that differentiated CORE members sharply from their white liberal "allies." For white CORE members, Negroes became the major reference group for all matters dealing with civil rights and with their political position generally. For many, the Negroes in CORE replaced all previous reference groups in importance, and the Negro reference group became decisive in the members' judgments of almost every aspect of life. The two main factors that brought this about were personal contact and Negro dominance of CORE groups.

All but three of the eighteen white respondents interviewed reported that they had formed very close personal friendships with Negroes as a result of their CORE activities.* These friendships included visiting in each other's homes, sharing social activities, and exchanging views and experiences on all subjects, including very personal ones. Above all, the members were involved in sharing the immensely absorbing work of the movement, which often eclipsed more usual or personal interests. Seven of the respondents had dating and love relationships with Negroes, and one was married to a Negro.

This close association with Negroes is very rare among white liberals outside the direct action movement. Contacts there are usually limited to cooperation on community projects, interracial committees, or political activities. Generally, these more conventional activities demand only partial involvement by the participants; therefore they are unlikely to

* The three who lacked such contact had an exceptionally low degree of involvement in their group, as measured by the amount of time spent in CORE activities and in offices held in the groups.

form the personal ties that grow out of a common wholly absorbing involvement. Close friendships or romantic attachments are seldom formed by persons older and more involved in their families, in their established friendships, and in the social ties within their own racial communities. Also, the older generation of Negro leaders, with whom such whites work, tend to block intimate personal contacts because of their greater fear and suspicion of whites.

The contrast between white direct actionists and white liberals who function outside the direct action movement is most striking in the South, where even very dedicated liberals have almost no organizational or personal ties with Negroes. The difference between these patterns of contact and the consequent outlook of whites was exemplified to the investigator during a field trip with a white, liberal, Northern-educated university professor who was teaching in a white Southern college. He had been actively engaged in struggles against segregationists in the city, yet his personal acquaintance with Negroes was limited to rather awkward semiannual professional encounters with his opposite number in the city's Negro college. During one of our conversations, he said to me, "I have to keep reminding myself that you actually associate with Negroes." The resulting difference in reactions—which should, by virtue of training, background, and general political commitment, have been very similar—came out sharply several times during the field trip.

We visited a small town in which demonstrations had taken place recently, and the atmosphere was so tense that we were afraid to ask directions in the white section of town. We succeeded, however, in contacting a Negro youth who had taken part in the demonstrations and who invited us to his home. At the end of the interview, my companion rose to examine a group of pictures on the mantelpiece. The respondent explained that one picture, that of a light-skinned young Negro girl in a graduation dress, was of his girl friend. My companion startled the respondent and myself greatly by asking quite innocently whether or not she was a white girl. I was acutely embarrassed by the naïveté of the question and was aware that our respondent had become alarmed and suspicious of us.

On a second occasion, after interviewing a local newspaper editor, we were completely unable to agree on the position to be imputed to this man. After the lynching of a fourteen-year-old Negro boy several years earlier, the editor had drawn down the wrath of some local segregationists by stating that the people of Mississippi were opposed to extremism of both kinds: lynchings and the NAACP. On this basis my companion defined him as a moderate who had courageously withstood extremist elements in his environment. During the interview, however, the editor described youthful civil rights demonstrators as subversives and sex perverts and held that whites should never yield to civil rights pressures. On this basis I defined him as a segregationist whose position could in no way be differentiated from that of the White Citizens Council. Doubtless, there were legitimate arguments on both sides of the question. But my definition of the editor, like my reaction to the question about the graduation picture, stemmed from an almost automatic awareness of how my Negro acquaintances would have reacted to the situation. These two incidents illustrate typical differences between white liberals and white direct actionists in the South.

The less extreme environment of the North produces subtler differences. But the extent to which close association with Negroes conditions whites to reactions that would be alien to most liberal whites is expressed in this anecdote related by a white Northern CORE member:

> The movement changes your outlook in a lot of little ways. The other day I stopped in a service station to use the restroom. I stuck my head inside the office where two white men were sitting and they told me that the "boy" repairing cars had the key. The "boy" was a grown Negro man, and I felt an immediate flash of anger. I said, "He's not a boy. Why can't you call him a man?" They were so startled they probably still haven't figured it out.

The decision to join direct action and the personal involvement with Negroes created for some members a situation that isolated them from the white community and forced them to live almost entirely within the Negro community. For instance, the Northern white respondent with a Negro husband had to live in the Negro ghetto, and she learned to share many of the reactions of Negroes in the area. A Southern woman in her thirties found that after joining CORE and acquiring a Negro boyfriend and other Negro friends she had little choice but to move into a Negro neighborhood and limit her contacts to Negroes and white CORE members.

Sociological literature on reference groups has paid relatively little attention to the importance of dominance and coercion in determining the influence of reference groups over the individual. Yet it is clear from our knowledge of child psychology that people have a deep need to identify with powerful figures and groups. In the long run, escape is the only alternative to accepting as a reference group a powerful, dominant group in one's immediate environment. It is not surprising, therefore, that the condition of CORE participation that forced whites to accept Negroes as a reference group was the fact that CORE groups were dominated—often numerically and almost always psychologically—by the Negro members.

One respondent, whose first contact with CORE was at a Southern CORE training institute, reported her growing awareness of this dominance and the effect it had on her self-evaluation:

> I remember that, when I went to the institute, I was feeling very gratified at myself for being such a crusader for other people's rights. But gradually I began to feel more and more uncomfortable with the role. The Negroes there did so much kidding about paternalistic whites, and how maybe we thought we were coming to "help our little brown brothers." They weren't nasty about it, but more sort of good-natured, as if we might probably be a little misled. I found myself wondering what they thought of me—and feeling afraid that maybe I was being condescending. Finally, I wanted to somehow escape from this role as "white ally" to find some reason why I had as much at stake as any Negro. I notice that some people who are Jewish try to trade on that—that they have had so much experience with prejudice that they have a real personal stake in this—but the Negroes don't buy this. You can't get off the hook that way.

White members came to feel that they were dependent on Negro members for genuine acceptance into the group. As one member put it:

> That's one reason you're in the movement. You want to define this situation as one we're all affected by as human beings—to get things to a point where you're not an outsider any longer.

Another white complained rather bitterly:

> Whether you find a role or not depends on the attitudes of the Negroes. It's up to them to accept you or not. Either they want you to work with them or they don't want you to work for them. What I mean is either they let you be part of a group

where everybody is working for integration or else you are whites, supporting them in getting rights for Negroes.

The feeling expressed in the last quotation is not a matter of abstract philosophical conviction. It stemmed out of a situation in which a white CORE member, although a local officer, was excluded from the inner circle of the group because it was awkward and sometimes dangerous to include him in all the informal socializing of the leadership clique. The Negro leaders of this Southern chapter were unwilling to risk difficulties with the police and other agencies just to safeguard the right of white members to share fully in its social and organizational life. The sense of exclusion felt by the white member was identical to that felt by most Negroes in white society: because of his race, he was cut off from privileges in which he was keenly interested and he was dependent for inclusion on the "charity" of the Negroes.

Finding themselves in the unusual situation of dominance over white persons, Negroes in CORE tended—though probably not consciously—to "tighten the screws" on their white compatriots in many subtle ways. In part, they undoubtedly used the CORE whites as an outlet for frustrations suffered in a white-dominated world. But this process of increasing the demands made on white CORE members also arose from deeper needs: CORE represented the one arena of social intercourse in which Negroes could "make good"—completely and without compromise—their demand for equal treatment and respect. The CORE groups were psychological testing grounds for the Negro's ability to assert his new self-image. The continual testing and prodding of whites was probably also an outgrowth of the deep desire of many Negro members to find a wholly dependable group who would spare them the embittering rancor and reverse racism created by previous contacts with whites.

A few examples of this process may be illuminating. One respondent told of this experience while working with a Southern CORE group:

I was living at the YWCA and didn't know many people in CORE well, so I used to eat downtown. One day I showed up at a CORE meeting with a matchbook from a downtown cafeteria. E got hold of it and said, "One of those segregated cafeterias, huh?" And I said weakly, "I have to eat somewhere." A little later he said, "I'm going to bring it up about these white CORE members at the next convention—coming down here and enjoying our segregated facilities. How are we ever going to get rid of them that way?" This was all in E's eternal leg-pulling manner. But it hit the mark.

Small wonder that most whites developed acute guilt about using such facilities and generally went to great lengths to avoid using them—even when their exclusion from the Negro community left them with no facilities at all. This taboo on using segregated facilities, it should be noted, was another way in which CORE whites differed sharply from other white liberals in the South.

At one national convention, I sat in on an informal discussion in which Northern Negro delegates told of very subtle insults suffered at their places of employment. One Negro nurse told with great bitterness of a very friendly white co-worker who committed the unforgivable faux pas of asking the Negro whether she knew of anyone who did domestic work. The white person who heard many such stories and was exposed to the Negroes' reaction to them soon realized that he might never be safe from making such a mistake and thus "acting like a white person."

Whites, depending on their personalities, responded to these pressures in varying ways: many reacted with open anger when they were accused of prejudice or when they were excluded from privileges and activities because of race; others completely accepted the guilt imputed to them. Extreme in his acceptance of this conditioning was one white Northern respondent who turned the pressure inward and searched within himself for the "remnants of racism":

Negroes always mistrust whites, even in CORE—it's understandable. The poison of racism exists in all of us. I live in the ghetto and find all the poverty and drunkenness and mental disorder. When you are face to face with it day by day, well, unless you pull yourself together you'll probably start making racial generalizations . . . One night I got quite drunk with a close Negro friend, and I guess it brought out his paranoia. He said to me, "I am trying to hate you but I can't—I know you too well. But you're the stereotype of a white Protestant and I hate you for the way you look." There is nothing one can do. It hurts me a little. But I've come to expect it. I questioned myself whether the distrust is justified. It is just. I'm not sure any Negro should ever trust any white. Whites haven't done enough to justify trust—it's too recent and too sudden.

There were many rewards as a result of white acceptance of Negroes as an authoritative reference group. The white CORE member who accepted the group's values usually succeeded in becoming an "insider." He was meted out the privileges of "Negroness." Without any feeling of being implicated, he could share in the jokes directed at the opposition. He could even laugh with impunity at the foibles of the "white liberals." He attained the right to judge individual Negroes in the group harshly and to criticize them freely. And for those who shared the feelings of the guilt-stricken respondent quoted above, there was the enormously gratifying experience of real trust, unity, and genuine human bonds across the racial line. The sharing of painful experiences such as injury and imprisonment often created a temporary atmosphere of complete unity. And on a more pedestrian level, the steady work in the group, the factional struggles—which seldom occurred along purely racial lines—and the appreciation that organizers had for the efficient all served to create an atmosphere in which the race factor became secondary to other ties, interests, likes, and dislikes.

The white CORE member's almost exclusive identification with Negro reference groups followed logically from his position in the power play of the various community groups. The white liberal functioning outside the direct action movement was typically engaged in a double-edged process of persuasion: trying to get his own racial community to accept more integration and trying to hold back Negro demands to a point where they would be accepted by the white community. He became a mediator and peacemaker between the two racial communities. The white CORE member, on the other hand, engaged in an open conflict situation: he and his organization pitted the strength of the Negro community against white defenders of the status quo.[1] Thus, the CORE white could not function as a middleman; by definition he had chosen to take sides with the Negro community.

The white CORE member chose a course that eventually created a deep gulf between himself and the ordinary white liberal. Lewis Killian describes the usual white liberal very clearly in the following passages:

> The white person, no matter how liberal he may be, exists in the cocoon of a white-dominated society. Living in a white residential area, sending his children to white schools, moving in exclusively white social circles, he must exert a special effort

to expose himself to the actual conditions under which large numbers of Negroes live. Even when such exposure occurs, his perception is likely to be superficial and distorted.[2]

While there is little that the Negro may do that does not remind him of his status as a Negro, the white man does not most of the time think of himself primarily as a white man. He thinks of himself instead in his other roles as a businessman, a parent, a teacher, a church member, a worker, a politician, or what have you. The Negro lives as an outsider in the white man's world. The white man, even though he may disapprove of it, is an insider in this world. For him to subject it to constant criticism on the basis of the single issue of racial values requires that he jeopardize other values. Hence, the white liberal is handicapped, whether he knows it or not, by a vested interest in the existing order.[3]

The significance of the conditioning process that the white CORE member underwent was precisely that: when he was fully socialized into the group, the above description no longer applied to him.

Ingroup Versus Outgroup

CORE's "definition of the world," the outlook learned by the white CORE member during his socialization into the group, was developed out of a mixture of some white and mostly Negro influences and reactions to experiences encountered in the course of direct action.

A crucial factor in any group's world view is the boundary it draws around itself, the borderline it recognizes between "we" and "they." In essence, when CORE members said "we," they meant only CORE and other direct action organizations. Rigorously excluded were the bulk of white liberals, "established Negro leaders," and the Negro community. Some white liberals and Negro leaders who were especially close to and supportive of CORE might, on occasion, be included in the "we," but this was relatively rare. More often, they were referred to as "people who will support us," "people who are sympathetic," and "the Negro community." What most sharply differentiated the "we" from the "they" was the willingness to use and the wholehearted endorsement of direct action as a useful and fitting device in nearly all circumstances. Thus, despite CORE's disapproval of his organization's general policy, a white official of the Catholic Interracial Council or the Unitarian church or a Negro minister could become a "we" person by virtue of being seen on CORE picket lines or by committing civil disobedience.

Direct action was clearly recognizable as an act that set the participant off in the eyes of the "respectable" Negro and white communities as well as in the eyes of the direct actionists themselves. CORE members recognized that members of other civil rights groups might often talk exactly like themselves about issues but might never take part in direct action. Among civil rights groups, the call to the picket line produced an immediate, physical, and clearly recognizable division of temperaments, orientations, and commitments.

For Negroes, this definition of "we" and "they" required some readjustment; the definition, for many of them, had previously been drawn entirely along racial lines. For whites, redefinition was more drastic, not because it was a problem to find oneself in a racially mixed ingroup, but because it was a distinct problem for the white member to learn that many of the white organizations, agencies, and leaders he had always considered friendly to civil rights were considered lukewarm or downright treacherous by CORE standards. The federal government, the liberal wing of the Democratic party, the AFL-CIO, and most churches were looked upon as groups that had to be prodded and pushed into taking civil rights stands. The white member also learned—partly through experience, but more through the learning of group definitions —that the police, the courts, the FBI, some unions, and some agencies he would have considered at least neutral on civil rights were considered outright opponents. One white CORE member, who received his initiation into CORE during a Southern training institute, recalled:

> One of the big shocks to me was how skeptical the Negroes at the institute were of the NAACP and the federal government, unions, and so forth. They made you feel that you were awfully naïve to even mention getting help from these groups. Another thing I remember being kidded about a great deal was my attitude that policemen were nice people who keep order and give you street directions. I learned that they were enemies of the movement and that police brutality against Negroes is a problem in every big city in the country.

As a result of this conditioning, white CORE members frequently found themselves in dispute with their white liberal and moderate friends of pre-CORE days. After a year in CORE, it was often shocking to them to find "how conservative their old friends had become." One member said:

> Friends of mine—kids who are liberal Democrats—were shocked by my attitude toward the administration. They're for civil rights, you know, but felt it was going a little too far. They have this "it's going to take time" attitude. I had found this attitude irritating before, but hadn't really thought about it. Contact with Negroes is important here. You see the dire needs for change and you get the feeling that it has to be immediate: "Freedom Now—it should have been yesterday."

Another member reported:

> I think being in CORE has made me less tolerant of others—not that I think that's bad, because I don't think these people deserve tolerance, people who are prejudiced. I'm even more intolerant of people who are conservative generally. I always was intolerant of people who were prejudiced. But I find now that where in the past I could like people if the subject of civil rights just didn't come up, now it has to come up—partly because I am so involved. And then if I find out that a person feels different I can't have a positive feeling for that person. I can't be nice to them.

If the neutrals and liberals came in for heavy criticism in the CORE definition of things, the "enemy," including both outright segregationists and "moderates," came in for fine dissection and ridicule. Certain stock claims of the conservatives, such as the claim that direct action increases racial tension or "disrupts racial harmony" or that it "alienates the moderates," were so constantly ridiculed that group members needed only to look at each other when such a remark was made to signal a common joke.

One of the most vivid ways in which the enemy, with his various characteristics and arguments, was satirized was in sociodramas held in the course of training for direct action and negotiations. Although training was the manifest function of these sociodramas, satirizing of the opponent and the creation of common definitions of the opponent were certainly major latent functions. Negroes usually took the lead in these satires and played white figures such as businessmen in sociodramas of negotiations and white hecklers in sociodramas of direct action. In the course of these rehearsals, white participants learned that a businessman was very likely to tell you that he had a wonderful "boy" employed in his firm—had

had him for forty years, as a matter of fact—and that this "boy," who was invariably the janitor, was one of his best friends. He was also likely to learn that if the negotiation involved employment problems, the employer was likely to confess a sudden and complete inability to tell anyone's race, by way of explaining why he could not supply racial breakdowns of his employees. When such remarks were made in the course of actual negotiations, the white members' adherence to the group's definitions was enormously strengthened. The group had predicted the enemy's behavior correctly and everyone already had an ingrained reaction that they knew was shared by other members of the negotiating team.*

Perception of the Race Problem Extended and Deepened

Through their association with Negro members, whites in CORE extended their perception of the civil rights problem into many new areas. They became aware of the extent of discrimination in housing, employment, public accommodations, public schools, labor unions, churches, social clubs, civil service, and police departments. Whites and Negroes in America perceive the same physical and social reality through such different glasses that things visible to one group are often totally invisible to the other. The white CORE member learned to look through the Negro's spectacles to the extent that his previous outlook became almost unimaginable to him.

It should be noted that in associating with CORE Negroes, the CORE whites were coming in contact with an exceptionally critical and outspoken group within the Negro community. Not infrequently, the CORE white became more sensitized to civil rights problems and more vehement in his opposition to segregation than the average, apolitical Negro. In addition, participation in the movement exposed members to direct conflict with police, political figures, businessmen, and segregationist citizens. A CORE member who had experienced

* This shared definition was also reassuring to Negro members, who knew that they were not alone in their reactions of annoyance and rage. One Negro member, for example, reported that during the course of a negotiation with an employer, the employer referred to his Negro employees as "boys." Neither he nor his white partner made an issue of it because they felt it would get the negotiations off the main point. But he said, "It was easier to pass over it because I knew that X [the white negotiator] would have caught it too and we would laugh about it afterwards."

arbitrary arrest, police brutality, and the like extended his social criticism far beyond the issue of segregation. He could probably never again look upon the general social system with trust, acceptance, or satisfaction. As one Southern-group member put it:

> My experiences in jail tended to make me cynical of local law—and I suppose with any metropolitan police force. It educated me to aspects of real politics that you can't get from reading. The sense of futility at being so arbitrarily treated as a criminal . . . Here were the forces of law and order I'd always assumed were here to protect me.

Another member, raised in the North but active in the South, described his first experience of disillusionment:

> When I first went to CORE meetings, I saw that nobody was really doing anything—I wanted to get into some kind of action right away. So I spoke up and said, "Let's picket Woolworth downtown." Everybody was afraid to go and thought we'd be arrested. But I said, "We're in America. We can't be arrested for that." I've seen people hand out leaflets and picket in New York all the time, so I didn't possibly expect to be arrested. Nobody would go, so finally I said, "All right, I'll go alone," and then one or two people decided to join me. Finally we had ten people volunteer. Well, we were picked up by the police after we had been there five minutes. I was outraged.

Not only did the white members' perception broaden out to criticisms of the whole social system, but the attitudes deepened, took on a more vital emotional coloring, and became deeply ingrained, powerful reactions. In subtle ways and by almost imperceptible little steps, the benefit of the doubt was shifted from the white to the Negro community. Whereas before joining CORE most members would have required strong proof of discrimination before fighting out a housing or employment case, after some time in CORE they were likely to feel that any claim of discrimination was valid until proven otherwise. From treating Northern discrimination as an exception, they moved to assuming its presence everywhere. From recognizing only outright refusals as discrimination, they came to include a patronizing manner or a slightly different requirement under their definition of discrimination.

Even the perception of and reaction to physical differences between the races were often altered. The way in which experience with segregationists could turn into an actual, and almost instinctive, dislike of white people in general was noted by this white CORE member working in the South:

> When handing out leaflets in a Southern city, you can almost always predict people's reactions by their race. When a white person comes toward me I steel myself for an insult or, at least, a rejection. When I see a Negro coming I feel relieved, because I know he's going to take my leaflet. After a while Negroes begin to look a lot kinder to you than white people, with their hard, set mouths. Once a group of us went to "swim-in" at a beach near here. I was really afraid of violence and my stomach was drawing into a knot all the way down. Near the beach we passed a Negro section of town and I felt a little leap of relief—here were friends, here might be a place to run to if we had to. There have been times when I've looked at some white men—the types that molest us—and I've felt a revulsion at their pasty white faces and watery blue eyes. They looked ugly to me, just the way they must look to Negroes.

Nonviolent Ideology

Thus far, we have been describing the process of radicalization that the white member underwent as a result of his contacts and experiences in CORE. Yet it might be hypothesized that the CORE philosophy of nonviolence worked as an ideological antidote, to keep the white member's growing sense of injustice within bounds that strictly prescribed the methods he might use in the struggle. As discussed earlier, the interviews show that whites were, indeed, much more likely than Negroes to develop an intellectual interest in the philosophy of nonviolence, to read about it, and to strive for consistency by broadening the application of nonviolence to problems of war and personal ethics. This tendency reflected the greater intellectual background of white members. Yet when the effect of radicalization is weighed against the influence of nonviolent philosophy, one finds that the influence of radicalization—although doubtless held in check by the philosophy of nonviolence—was the stronger. Fourteen of our eighteen respondents gave sufficiently complete answers to be evaluated on this question.

Six of these fourteen persons had formed definite opinions on the question of nonviolence before coming in contact with CORE. Two were convinced pacifists and four were radicals who questioned the advisability of nonviolence as a commitment for the movement. None of these six were affected by the CORE version of nonviolence, and none changed their original positions during their contact with CORE.

The other eight respondents reported that nonviolence was "not an issue" to them before joining CORE. In evaluating their development, we must realize that the opinion described as "nonviolence is not an issue" automatically assumes that Negroes *should not* use violence in their movement —the usual attitude of white Americans. The question of nonviolence simply never becomes a conscious issue. The act of consciously asking, "Should Negroes use violence to attain their ends?" is already a decidedly radicalizing step in the development of an individual's thinking—even when that violence is conceived of in purely defensive terms. Thus, when we find that six of the eight respondents who started from this position continued to accept nonviolence for the movement, we must conclude that they did not change their position as far as outward commitment to action was concerned. A subtle point, perhaps impossible to resolve, is whether in the minds of these persons a commitment to moderation was strengthened because the philosophy of nonviolence had been partially absorbed or whether the first step toward radicalism had been taken because the very question "Should the Negro use violence?" had been implicitly raised, even though answered for the moment in the negative. We may speculate that the three persons who reported a deep intellectual interest in nonviolent philosophy had strengthened their commitment, while the three who only adopted it as a tactic may have become implicitly more radical by having considered the alternative.

Only two of the fourteen respondents reported a clear change in position. Both said that before joining CORE, nonviolence was not an issue. However, both came to question nonviolence—one, after studying the philosophy, had this influence counteracted by the radicalizing influences in CORE; the other, after being exposed to the radicalizing influences, was unaffected by and uninterested in CORE's philosophy of nonviolence.

In summary, those who questioned nonviolence upon entering the movement were not won to positions of nonviolence, and some of those who implicitly accepted nonviolence came to question it as a result of participation in the movement. The majority had seemingly not changed their outward commitment, leaving us to speculate on the underlying changes that may have taken place.

Why did the philosophy of nonviolence have so little effect on the ideological development of white CORE members? The white members' initial reaction upon joining CORE was usually great enthusiasm about the idea of nonviolence. During this "nonviolent honeymoon" the philosophy loomed large as a way of legitimating a new and questionable role and appealed to the idealism that brought many people to the movement. Two members described their initial reactions:

> Nonviolence made a great impression when I joined. At the time, I felt that pacifism was a goal I desired, and I wanted to be able to call myself a pacifist. Before CORE I was a pretty violent person. After joining, I read Gandhi's *Non-Violent Resistance* and two biographies of him and all the peace literature that came my way. I think it would take self-questioning and self-discipline to call oneself a pacifist.

> I thought it was an excellent idea when I came into the organization—wonderful that this organization had a new philosophical idea behind it. At that time everyone was thinking about it and it was an inner thing. Everyone was reading Gandhi's biography and his speeches and writings. It became an active discussion point at meetings. But it isn't there any more. I mean nonviolence is still there, but not the philosophical idea behind it—that's gone. Everything has become so businesslike—I mean, now they are negotiating and they know exactly what to do.

In the closing statement above we find a hint of why the initial enthusiasm for nonviolence died down. First, CORE was shifting the emphasis from the philosophical aspects of nonviolence to a commitment to nonviolence merely as a strategy. Second, and partly in explanation of this development, the Negro majority that came to dominate most groups was not, in the main, interested in nonviolence as a philosophy and ethic. Extensive intellectual discussion of the point was not encouraged. Indeed, the sensitive white member usually began to feel that an exaggerated interest in nonviolence marked him off as not quite militant. Gradually he learned to accept the Negro version of nonviolence, which merged the concept with discipline, courage, and militancy and generally emphasized the latter to the detriment of such gentle and inward characteristics of nonviolence as forgiveness, inner purity, and genuine goodwill toward the "foe."

As important as the influence of Negro CORE members were the experiences to which white members were exposed in the course of direct action—experiences that not only lead the member to question nonviolence but lead to a general disillusionment with the standard version of political morality they had accepted before joining the movement. As one member put it:

> Before I got to dealing with employers on these negotiations, I would never have dreamed that businessmen would lie right to your face the way they do. Also, we have found that all your moral arguments roll off them like water off a duck's back. But put a dent in their cash register and all of a sudden they discover the moral issues. Another thing I've found by being involved in some lawsuits: in court everybody lies. All the lawyers lie and encourage all the witnesses to lie. There is darned little morality behind the scenes.

Another respondent, chairman of a Northern chapter, said:

> When we first started working on employment, the white members always wanted to bring about a change in employment policy, and the Negro members wanted to ask for the hiring of specific numbers. I finally learned to do it their way because if you don't give these businessmen something specific to live up to, they don't even know what you mean by a change of policy. You can only push them—like the political leaders, you don't change their minds. I've never seen any changing of hearts. There isn't much talk about that any more in our chapter.

Thus, through direct experience in the power struggle, as well as through the interpretation of the morality of white power holders given by the more cynical Negro members, the white member gradually learned to interpret the situation more and more as a *naked power struggle* and less and less in terms of moral example and conversion.* Frequently, the white member was left with a feeling of ambivalence. He

* For the Negro member, by contrast, it was often surprising to see the white community "really acting on principle." The following quote by a Southern Negro expresses this view: "One of the things that has really taken me by surprise is this. We always saw the white man making money —wherever there was a buck he knew how to get it. If there was something new to open, he'd open it—and they let the Negroes spend their money there. I grew up with this feeling. Recently, the whites have lost money over this and that really fooled me. In basketball, for instance, if they let just two halfway good Negroes play they would pack the stadium. But they don't do it cause I guess they really believe in segregation."

found moral inspiration in nonviolence, but he found it wanting as an interpretation of reality. This ambivalence is well expressed by this "disappointed lover of nonviolence":

> My views broadened out in favor of nonviolence in a broader sense than just physical nonviolence. It broadened out for me in terms of human relations. On the other hand, I have drifted away from it—I mean, now the use of violence in political conflicts. I've seen situations where I think violence could have exerted more positive influence than nonviolence. What has also led me away from it is getting a broader view of the segregation problem, for example, local police brutality. I think it could be challenged by a violent action more successfully than by nonviolence. I see that violence in the past has sometimes exerted real impetus to improving the situation of the Negro, as do some race riots on a large scale.

Finally, the importance of nonviolence for the white CORE member waned as he became more absorbed in his CORE-Negro reference group and more divorced from his former white reference groups. With the new image of American society provided by CORE Negroes he had less need of an elaborate justification for direct action.

Whites and Negroes on Questions of Nonviolence and General Radicalism

In the discussion of the relationship between commitment to nonviolence and general radicalism, it was shown that whites tended to be somewhat less radical than Negroes on the "moderation-radicalism typology" (the position on nonviolence in the movement plus the position on the use of nonviolence in national defense). They were also less polarized than Negroes. For purposes of this discussion, let us reconsider the data tabulated in Chapter 7.

	Negro	White
Moderate	6	1
Nonviolent	8	7
Radical	7	3

The polarization of Negro opinion, it will be recalled, was due to the striking differences between the moderation of the Southern Negro members and the radicalism of the Northern Negro members. White members were not markedly different in the two regions. Most Southern white members were from the same left-to-liberal milieu that produced most Northern white militants. Hence, it is clear that in the Southern chapters whites were more radical than Negroes and probably provided a radicalizing influence, whereas in the Northern chapters whites were more moderate than Negroes and exerted a moderating influence. Other measures of radicalism yield the same picture. In Southern chapters white members were more critical of the American system and more supportive of black nationalist attacks on the system than were Negro members. In Northern chapters, on the other hand, whites were less critical of the United States and less supportive of black nationalism than were their Negro counterparts.*

Looking closely at patterns of opinion among whites and Negroes, we find a difference in ideological syndromes and political styles that does not show up in our quantified interview data. There were several Negro respondents who ranked as radical in their attitude toward the use of nonviolence in the movement yet did not show high scores on criticism of the American system. These were older, working class persons whose education and political experience were below the group average. They simply were not very verbal and gave little detail on any matters covered in the interview. These "nonverbal radicals" represent a political style quite common in the Negro community, and Negro CORE members reflected this style in the narrow focus of their political interest. Even most of those who were extremely outraged and dissatisfied tended to limit their political perspective to the race question.

Nonverbal radicals were wholly absent from our white group. In this group, there was a small number who were atypical in that they were critical of American society but supported nonviolence in the movement. Most of their criti-

* The extent to which Northern whites actually voiced their opinions and thus functioned to moderate Negro radicalism may be exaggerated by these findings from the interviews. Throughout this analysis, I was troubled by a seeming contradiction between the interview data and the impressions gathered at Northern chapter meetings. There, it had seemed that, in discussions of specific issues, whites took the radical position about as frequently as did Negroes. I am indebted to Horace Cayton for suggesting what seems a very plausible explanation of this contradiction: the interviewer was white, therefore the desire to appear sufficiently radical before the Negro reference group—a motive that operated to determine white behavior at meetings—may have been inoperative in the interviews.

cisms were based on the "radicalism of nonviolence"—a political style found in mild form in only one of our Negro respondents. Those whites who were both critical of America and skeptical about nonviolence generally voiced comprehensive criticisms of the society involving at least some traditional Marxist themes.

In general, it may be said that Negro radicalism in CORE tended to be sharper and more bitter but also more narrowly focused than the radicalism of whites. It seldom extended to broad analyses of society on pacifist, Marxist, or other philosophical bases. It revolved around the one problem of race and usually arose out of direct experience rather than theoretical considerations. White radicalism was somewhat more muted by nonviolent commitments. It was less extreme and sharp yet was broader, more inclusive of other issues, and more consistent. Whites brought to the movement critical theories about American society. They took from it a new sense of outrage born of deep personal involvement with Negroes in the movement and extensive personal experience in the day-to-day encounter between the direct-actionists and the business leaders, political leaders, police, and prison wardens of the community.

NOTES

1. For an excellent discussion of the persuasive and conflicting relationships, see Lewis Killian and Charles Grigg, *Racial Crisis in America: Leadership in Conflict* (Englewood Cliffs, N.J.: Prentice-Hall, 1946), pp. 99 ff.
2. *Ibid.*, p. 73.
3. *Ibid.*, p. 95.

CHAPTER 10

Weaknesses of the
Nonviolent Commitment

Gandhi distinguished between genuinely nonviolent movements, whose primary commitment is to nonviolent means,
and passive resistance movements, whose primary commitment
is to the attainment of a political end and whose use of nonviolent means continues only as long as they are too weak
to use violence. In this sense, CORE was essentially a passive
resistance movement. However deep may have been the nonviolent commitment during CORE's earliest years and however serious and absolute may have been the pacifism of some
of its members and leaders, the overwhelming majority who
made up the movement after 1961 were primarily dedicated
to one end: civil rights. The commitment to nonviolence was
not only shallow but also weak, for it rested on psychological
foundations that were destined to be eroded away by the
progress of the movement itself.

The doctrine of nonviolence is essentially alien to American culture. It had an enormous appeal to the civil rights
movement because it could legitimate the seemingly drastic
tactic of direct action; the movement needed no elaborate
ideology to justify its goals because its demands fitted very
readily into the official American creed of human equality.
Whereas the goals required no defense, the tactics needed
elaborate justification. This need for vindication was not due
mainly to the radical nature of direct action tactics, for the
labor movement had used similar tactics with impunity. The
basic reason for this necessity was the enormous gap between
the official American creed and the actual practices and private attitudes. It arose from the very extent and depth of the
"American dilemma." On the part of most whites, there has
always been an underlying assumption of Negro inferiority—
pervasive and powerful, even though frequently denied. As a
creature of American culture, the Negro shared these assumptions. His doubt about his human equality was fed not only

by the dominant white society but also by the cultural weaknesses within Negro society.* Whites and Negroes might agree verbally that a Negro has the same right to equal treatment as a white man, but both actually found it much more defensible for a white man to fight for his rights by demonstrating or picketing—or by shooting back at someone who was shooting at him.

The doctrine of nonviolence begged the question of equality in that it denied the reality of the movement's coercive power and in fact limited the actual coercion that could be used by its members. Behind its pronouncement that "no man should use violence" lurked the popular notion that "the Negro should not use violence." As has been shown, many members of the movement used the former notion to explain the movement's renunciation of self-defense while advocating violence in national self-defense without being conscious of any contradiction. In its glorification of the Negro as the bearer of a new and morally superior political ethic, the doctrine tried to compensate for the common assumption of Negro inferiority, saying, in effect, "Give us the same rights you have because we are better than you," an argument used only by those who believe that they are not quite as good.

Given this basic function of the nonviolent doctrine, the very successes of the movement were destined to undermine the commitment to nonviolence. Direct action enabled Negroes to confront and defeat white power holders in a very direct and personal way. The experience of success and of wielding power acted as a powerful tonic, bracing the members with a new feeling of confidence. In the analysis of radicalism within the movement, it was shown that the highest-status Negroes, those who had experienced the greatest success and equality, were the most willing to question the commitment to nonviolence because the experience of equality raises expectations faster than society is usually able to deliver. Upward mobility increases the level of relative deprivation, that is, the gap between expectation and reality. Obviously, the same logic applies to the psychological effect that the movement's successes have on its members and on Negroes gen-

* I refer here to the fact that Negroes were the only minority in America whose original culture was almost totally lost and who were forced to build a subculture entirely out of adaptations from the culture that defined them, their history, and their African origins in wholly negative terms.

erally. As the movement removes the Negro's doubt about his basic equality, it erodes the psychological underpinnings that support his commitment to nonviolence.

Nonviolence functioned brilliantly as a legitimation and glorification of the Negro for those predominantly Southern Negroes and white allies of the movement who were still deeply ambivalent about the Negro's right to equality. The ideology's weakness was that precisely to the extent that it appealed to those elements it lost its appeal for those who were shedding their doubts. Because the movement had never really challenged the acceptance of violent means in American culture, it was impossible for it to transform the nonviolent role into one of complete dignity and manhood. Physical strength and material power are simply too much a part of the society's view of human dignity to be turned lightly into their opposites. Thus, to the extent that nonviolence succeeded in apologizing for direct action, it failed to provide a satisfying self-image for the more radical Negro. It could not compete with the black nationalists, who offered an image of strength more congenial to the American tradition. The more successfully the movement demonstrated that the Negro was a man like any other man, the more insufferable became the limitations that the nonviolent philosophy placed upon the full expression of that manhood as defined in the culture.

Nonviolence failed also as a satisfactory explanation of the situation in which the movement found itself. The movement had pictured American racism as a shallow hangover from the past and had taught that racism could be cured on the level of moral appeal to the opponent. Never having developed any thorough analysis of the economic, social, and political factors, it treated both Southern and Northern segregation as if both were amenable to piecemeal reform. It thus failed to prepare the activists psychologically for the stubborn white resistance that materialized as soon as the white community recovered from the disorientation into which it had been thrown by the initial onslaught of direct action.

With these weaknesses, the nonviolent philosophy was destined to fail as an ideology that could give meaning to the efforts and sacrifices demanded by a prolonged and often bloody struggle. Whatever the effect of nonviolent tactics on the overall amount of white violence, there were countless situations in which nonviolence increased the immediate physical dangers faced by the activists. Risking death must, psychologically, be for ultimate values, and nonviolence, as it functioned in the direct action movement, was never really raised to the level of an ultimate value.

Direct action was adopted as a strategy at a time when the civil rights movement felt that its push for progress through institutional political channels had been effectively blocked. The major reason why these channels could not be used was that they were controlled by the white majority, which was unwilling to see basic changes in the system of segregation. Even the courts officially independent of such majority pressure, became relatively powerless to change conditions in the face of the unwillingness of the executive to enforce their decisions.

Had the movement failed to find a new strategy at this point, it might easily have turned toward the development of a broadly critical, revolutionary ideology or toward racial separatism accompanied by a complete rejection of white society. Such developments would probably not have produced changes in real conditions. But radical ideologies are often used as psychological substitutes for real power and real results by movements whose aspirations are effectively frustrated.

Frustrations that might have led to deep alienation were prevented as a new and promising outlet for activity opened up. Instead of contemplating their failure and debating the virtues and vices of American society late into the night, Negro students and white radicals were busy discussing the technicalities of investigation, negotiation, picketing, bail money, and publicity. Instead of countering political weakness with that sense of control provided by an all-explaining ideology, young Negroes overcame their sense of weakness and futility by directly confronting and defeating the white restaurant owner and the sidewalk heckler. The process of direct action provided an extremely satisfying, though perhaps sometimes misleading, sense of concrete progress. Unlike political action that hopes for some eventual breakthrough, direct action had its immediate feedback: it was possible to count the number of lunch counters desegregated and the number of jobs opened to Negroes. The utopia did not have to be projected into the far future. Little tangible bits of it were provided in the here and now, not so much in the enjoyment of new facilities—because these were still regarded as merely symbolic of the eventual goal—but in the sense of strength and exhilaration that a member could draw from participating in a unified, disciplined group effort that confronted the white community with the new image of the militant, self-assured Negro.

The direct action strategy was tremendously successful, but it contained some very important limitations. As we have shown, direct action brings about changes faster than they can be brought about through conventional political channels that depend upon the evolution of a new consensus on race relations. It does so by putting economic pressures on specific targets while largely sidestepping the problem of persuading the majority of the white community. Obviously the working of this strategy depends upon the tolerance of the majority in permitting it to function and upon the success of liberal and federal leadership in promoting acceptance of civil rights reforms in the white community. As direct action pushes the society further and further beyond what it finds acceptable, the majority becomes impatient and mobilizes repressive forces against direct action.

By 1964 white reaction against the direct action movement was already making itself felt. The increasingly heavy sentences being meted out for civil disobedience in the North, the Goldwater campaign, with its accompanying rightward shift in both parties, and the repeal of open-housing legislation in several states were symptoms of this growing white resistance. How much further the movement could succeed in pushing the white majority was not yet clear, but the extravagant hopes raised by the early successes of direct action were already growing dimmer.

Another weakness was that direct action was best suited to campaigns for equal service and employment in retail services and public accommodations. Here, boycott pressures and legal issues could be used to greatest effect. The broader problems of unemployment, slum clearance, public housing, and improvement of schools were less amenable to the direct action approach. Inevitably, then, the movement directed itself toward goals of interest to Southern Negroes for whom public accommodations was a pressing issue and to Northern middle class Negroes for whom white-collar employment and the opening of suburban housing were important issues. The average Northern ghetto inhabitant had little to gain from these activities.

These limitations on the direct action strategy meant that by 1964 the movement again was confronted by the alternatives of either developing new strategies or seeing itself brought to a standstill. As one contemplates the developments that have occurred since 1964—the decrease of direct action and the move toward ghetto organization, the abandonment of nonviolence and the increasing radicalization of the movement's ideology—questions arise: Are we seeing the development of new and effective strategies in the struggle for equality? Or are we witnessing a retreat—one in which an increasingly radical rhetoric is being used to hide that fact that the movement has been stopped once again by the overwhelming obstacle of white majority opinion?

EPILOGUE: End of Nonviolence

Political Action and Political Separatism

During 1964–1965 CORE supported the unsuccessful efforts of the SNCC-led Mississippi Freedom Democratic party to challenge and replace the regular white Mississippi delegation at the Democratic convention and to block the seating of the Mississippi congressmen in the House of Representatives. If the MFDP was, for all practical purposes, a Negro party, this was due to white racist attitudes and not to any purposeful desire for separation. The whole point of the party's campaign was to gain entry into the all-white Democratic party in the South.

By 1966 the mood of SNCC-led Negro voters' groups in the South was becoming more radical. In several Alabama counties where Negroes had large absolute majorities in the population, SNCC launched a third-party movement, whose emblem was a springing black panther. The "Black Panther" parties in these counties refused to take part in the Democratic primaries and prepared to enter their own independent slate of candidates in the 1966 elections. They rejected all coalition with moderate Democrats on a statewide level and announced their determination to use their majorities in order to take complete control of their county governments.

In 1966, as part of SNCC's shift toward greater militancy, its chairman, John Lewis, was replaced by Stokely Carmichael.[1] Lewis, a young Negro minister, was close to Martin Luther King and, though a frequent critic of the administration, was committed to a coalition with liberal forces in the Democratic party. Carmichael rejected coalition with Democrats, national or local. Asking Alabama Negroes to reform the Democratic party was, he said, like asking Jews to reform the Nazi party.[2] "The Democratic party in this country," said Carmichael, "is the most treacherous enemy of the Negro."[3]

Joining the black nationalists in their rejection of integration as a goal for Negroes, Carmichael called for a drive for economic and political power—"black power"—saying that "the reason the Negro is in the position he's in today is not because he's not integrated, but because he doesn't have power. Integration is an insidious subterfuge for white supremacy." [4]

Moves toward an independent all-Negro party began in the North with the organization of the Freedom Now party by Jesse Gray, the Reverend Milton Galamison, and other New York leaders in 1962. These men represented a position more radical than that of CORE and most organized civil rights groups. Their efforts met with little success as liberals and radicals rallied around the Democratic party to meet the threat of Goldwater's candidacy.

In June, 1964, another small beginning was made when Malcolm X, former Muslim leader, broke away from that organization to found the Organization for Afro-American Unity, whose goals included organizing Negroes into cohesive and politically independent voting blocs. More significant than the new organization was the philosophy that Malcolm brought to the political arena. Malcolm had broken with the Muslims primarily because he rejected the apolitical stance of withdrawal into all-Negro communities. This rejection was based not on any desire for integration but on the practical recognition that black communities are controlled by white politicians and white businessmen. Malcolm concluded that without a frontal assault on the power situation, there would be no real improvement in the ghetto. He brought to his new political activism the perspective of black nationalism. He urged his followers to recognize that they were not Americans but victims of Americanism.[5] Negroes who looked to the white leadership of America for rescue were kidding themselves. Malcolm advised them to shift their perspective to a world level, where nonwhites constitute an overwhelming majority:

> The only alternative that the black man has in America today is to take it out of Senator Dirksen's and Senator Eastland's and President Johnson's jurisdiction and take it downtown on the East River and lay it before that body of men who represent international law, and let them know that the human rights of black people are being violated . . .[6]

Like the Muslims and leftists, he identified the Negro protest movement with anticolonialist movements and, specifically, anticapitalist movements. Colonialism and racism were inextricably bound up with capitalism. Malcolm concluded, "You can't have capitalism without racism . . ." [7]

Malcolm assailed the doctrine of nonviolence and defended black nationalism as a "reaction to racism":

If we react to white racism with a violent reaction, to me that's not black racism. If you come to put a rope around my neck and I hang you for it, to me that's not racism. My reaction is the reaction of a human being reacting to defend himself and protect himself.[8]

Malcolm was assassinated in February, 1965, but he greatly influenced Northern Negro activists in spite of the brevity of his career. His significance, like that of Robert Williams, lay in the fact that he brought elements of nationalist and leftist thinking to bear on practical and immediate problems of the power struggle. He had begun to translate the highly appealing doctrine of black separatism into an ideology for political action.

Until 1964 CORE had an official policy of political neutrality, but during the Goldwater campaign and in the years following, it moved increasingly toward political involvement. CORE members and chapters took unofficial part in the 1964 campaign. In April, 1965, sixteen New York CORE chapters openly opposed Robert Wagner's reelection for mayor. The national CORE convention of that summer changed CORE's official policy to allow for partisan political activity.[9] The turn from exclusive dependence on direct action to involvement in election campaigns reflected the growing numerical strength of registered Negro voters (Southern registration drives had added 2 million Negroes to the voter rolls[10]), as well as the realization that the white majority was using the ballot to counteract changes that direct action had forced on the white population, North and South. Ominous in this respect was the "Proposition 14" campaign in California. During 1963 the California State Legislature, spurred in part by continuous direct action demonstrations, passed a law forbidding discrimination in the sale or rental of homes. In November, 1964, the law was put to a direct vote of the electorate under California's referendum provision. Despite the support of most clergymen, prominent citizens, and most leaders of both parties, the new housing law was overwhelmingly repealed by the voters.

At its 1966 convention, CORE developed its political action program further in the direction of political independence begun by Galamison, Malcolm X, and SNCC-sponsored groups in Mississippi and Alabama. The slogan "black power" was raised with special reference to the organization of Negro voting blocs, independent of both major parties. It was felt that such blocs could drive a hard bargain with both parties in return for Negro support and could act as an independent third force, especially in local elections.

The Shift from Direct Action to Community Organization

Beginning in 1964, CORE began to shift its emphasis from direct action to organizing the Negro ghetto. The riots that broke out during the summers of 1964 and 1965 brought home to CORE leaders their almost total lack of effective contact in the ghetto. CORE's ambivalent relationship to the lower class masses of the ghetto was dramatized by its role in the Harlem riot. A Negro teen-age youth had been shot by a white policeman, and CORE organized a protest demonstration against police brutality. Violence broke out when police moved barricades around the demonstrators and arrested the leaders of the march. Once underway, the riot was, of course, completely out of the control of any organized group. Some CORE leaders toured the area trying to restore order, but they found themselves unable to curb the outbreak because they had very few organizational roots among the potential and actual rioters.

The riots came at a time when the earlier campaigns to desegregate public accommodations and open voter registration were drawing to a successful close. The civil rights bill had been passed. Negro communities in the South were making amazing progress in voter registration and political organization, and the Voting Rights Bill of 1965 held out new hope for successful registration drives in previously hard-core Deep South areas. Simultaneously, the situation in the Negro ghettos of the Northern cities was growing worse. Since the end of World War II, the number of chronically unemployed Negroes had been disproportionately high. As a result, the gap between white and Negro incomes, which had decreased substantially during the war, began to widen again.[11] Between 1960 and 1963 the percentage of white family income earned by the Negro fell from 55 percent to 53 percent.[12] Young people were particularly hard hit. In many Northern ghettos 60 to 70 percent of youths between sixteen and twenty-one were out of school and out of work.[13] There were also no significant gains in education and housing. California, Washington, and Michigan repealed open-occupancy legislation. In the field of education, the Supreme Court ruled that the reasoning of *Brown vs. Board of Education* did not apply to Northern de facto school segregation resulting from segregated housing patterns.[14]

Although most direct action groups had small membership in the ghetto, the victories of the movement raised the hopes of the Northern Negro poor. But although expectations were rising, the real situation did not improve. As a result, the ghettos began to explode into violence. The major outbreaks —Birmingham, 1963; Rochester and Harlem, 1964; Watts, 1965; Chicago and Cleveland, 1966—were accompanied by lesser outbreaks in smaller cities. Everywhere, CORE leaders found, as they had found in Harlem, that they could not control this violence, nor could they feel that their direct action activities had thus far brought any real improvement in the lives of ghetto residents. Most CORE projects had helped only the Southern Negro or the Northern middle class Negro. The problems of slums, police brutality, and, most important, unemployment had not yet really been touched.

The theme of the 1964 CORE convention at Durham, North Carolina, was "The Black Ghetto: An Awakening Giant." At this meeting, CORE leaders mapped out a new strategy. The main energy of the organization was to be redirected into community organization in the ghetto. Community centers, work training, political organization of welfare recipients, and similar projects were planned to build up a real lower class membership and to attack directly the economic, social, and political problems of the masses of Negro poor.[15] The convention also passed a constitutional amendment to give Negro community organizations connected with CORE a voice at future conventions.[16] This change reflected a recognition of the fact that the all-Negro community groups were far more congenial to most lower class Negroes than the typical, integrated CORE chapters.

The 1966 convention in Baltimore pushed this tendency further. In a recommendation to the convention, the national director of organizations, Herb Calendar, suggested that the older CORE groups should constitute themselves "supporters" and "resource persons" for ghetto organization. The suggestion underlined the new tendency to weaken the role of the established local CORE chapters, with their predominantly middle class and partially white membership. This shift in

CORE's make-up was reflected at Baltimore, where the delegates were about three-fourths Negro and had been recruited more heavily than ever before from the lower class ghetto.

At the same time that concentration on ghetto organization was weakening white influence in CORE, middle class Negro leaders were groping for an effective language with which to reach the Negro masses. Black nationalism had always had a natural appeal here. The average lower class Negro was much too far removed from the white middle class to be interested in integration. His problems were unemployment, low pay, overpriced poor housing, and inadequate schools. Further, his identity problem—the problem of self-hatred—could hardly be solved through proving himself according to the standards of middle class society. Reverse racism and the development of a positive, strong group consciousness was within easier reach. With this potential constituency in mind, CORE's national director, James Farmer, raised the question "Must we renounce ourselves and our community for the sake of integration?" [17] He answered the question by saying that "perhaps we . . . were at fault for not knowing sooner that some form of nationalism, or group-ism or ethnocentrism—there is no suitable name yet for this model I am trying to describe—can be incorporated into CORE's inner life without fatally compromising its ultimate ideals." [18]

The turn toward community organization in the Northern ghetto took part of its impetus from the federal poverty program. All over the country, local civil rights leaders were offered jobs with poverty program projects, and civil rights groups applied for federal funds to launch their own projects. As the inevitable struggle developed between the ghettos and the city administrations for control of the funds and projects of the poverty program, CORE activists played their role as insurgent leaders of the poor, demanding representation of the poor on poverty boards and fighting attempts of city and county agencies to gain control over the programs. The government had undoubtedly hoped to use the poverty program to dampen radical outbreaks and divert the energies of civil rights leaders from direct action and politics to community organization. The civil rights leaders, on the other hand, hoped to gain enough control over the funds to channel them into projects designed to politicize lower class Negroes and organize them to fight at all governmental levels for increased power and advantage. By 1966 it was as yet too early to tell which side was gaining its objectives in the uneasy alliance.

The major impetus for CORE's shift toward greater radicalism come from within the Negro community: the drive toward independent Negro politics in the South; the appeal of black nationalism, coupled with CORE's growing need to appeal to the ghetto in its own language; and finally, the increasing radicalism among American Negroes caused, in large part, by the very successes of the movement, which had raised expectations faster than it was able to change reality. An additional, though more peripheral, source of the changes in CORE was the emergence of the "new left" among the new generation of student activists.

Influence of the New Left

By the 1960s, the various old left and liberal groups, from social democrats to Americans for Democratic Action and the AFL-CIO, had become fairly conservative relative to American conditions. Organization of industrial unions, New Deal reforms, and general outlines of the welfare state, which had been the radical program of these groups in the 1930s and 1940s, were all firmly established. The Democratic party, carrier of these reforms, had been the ruling party, almost without interruption, for three decades.* Although all these groups enthusiastically supported the new civil rights movement, they saw it as the last necessary reform of an otherwise well-functioning system. They assumed that labor and the liberal Democrats were the natural allies of the Negro against the common enemies: Dixiecrat segregationists, conservative industrialists, and right-wing Republicans.

CORE emerged within this political constellation. During its early development it was strongly influenced by social democrats like James Farmer and Bayard Rustin, who were firmly anticommunist † and strongly identified with the liberal

---

* Even the once-revolutionary Communist party had turned to a practically conservative policy of coalition with established liberal groups and Democratic party organizations.

† CORE's constitution contains a phrase that is interpreted as excluding communists from membership. As recently as 1965, CORE fired one of its organizers for attending a Du Bois club strategy meeting. See "CORE Discloses Ouster of Its Mid-West Secretary," *The New York Times*, June 3, 1965, p. 23.

wing of the Democratic party. But the alliance with the liberal establishment has always been a somewhat uneasy one and has often come in for bitter criticism for its compromises with racism. The administration was openly assailed for its failure to provide adequate federal protection in the South and its appointment of racist judges to federal courts.[19] Until 1965, however, CORE was still firmly allied with these political forces, although disillusionment was developing rapidly within the ranks.

The groups that were most prominently identified with the emergence of the new left were the Students for a Democratic Society, an organization devoted to a broad range of domestic and foreign policy concerns, organized in 1960; the Student Nonviolent Coordinating Committee, which grew out of the 1960 sit-ins; and the Free Speech Movement, which developed at the University of California at Berkeley in 1964–1965. Crucial in the thinking of this new political generation was its identification of the liberal establishment as the major enemy: it seemed obvious that power—and therefore the responsibility for segregation, poverty, and a reactionary foreign policy—lay with the Democrats, the liberals, and organized labor, not with the Dixiecrats and reactionaries. As a new left spokesman put it, "My own disenchantment with the U.S. didn't really come because of its failures in Negro rights and foreign policy, but with the realization . . . that responsibility for these things lies with the most respectable people in society." [20]

To the new left, there was something basically wrong with the whole structure of a society in which the individual abdicated his power to large bureaucratic structures over which he had no control. The forms of parliamentary democracy were seen as wholly illusory: ". . . the enemy is 'corporate liberalism.' Existing institutions, from the Cold War to welfare, have been framed and are administered by political liberals who assume that the large corporation is the most desirable unit for organizing social and economic life." [21]

By 1965 the new left was characterizing America as "the most flexible of totalitarianisms, in which nearly all human activity is paralyzed in dependence on welfare capitalism and the cold war." [22]

The answer to bureaucratic control was "participatory democracy." Through direct action against bureaucracies and through the building up of parallel structures, such as "free universities," individuals could revolutionize society and regain control of their own institutions and destinies.

Whereas both the liberals and the old communist left had hoped to spread material benefits to the deprived, the followers of the new left questioned the whole quality of life in a materialistic society. They saw the abundance of material goods as an elaborate system of bribes through which the bureaucrats prevented the masses from controlling their own destinies.[23]

From their experience in the civil rights movement, the activists of the new left took the insight that the society was basically both racist and unable to solve the Negro's most crucial economic problems. The administration's war on poverty was seen as another typical ploy in the game of control from above:

> . . . Johnson's Great Society program . . . is an exercise in tokenism—part of the general strategy of the announced intention to "get the movement out of the streets while attempting to hold the black voter, the unemployed and others within the political confines of that rather unique trap—called the two-party system." [24]

As the struggle between city politicians and the representatives of the poor developed in cities across the nation and was resolved by Washington—usually in favor of the city machines —the warning of the new left began to find echoes in CORE: "The people are asking for jobs while we appoint washed up politicians and 'Negro leaders' to poverty jobs which means that they can now get paid to sit among the unpaid and show them the proper way to eat at the table." [25]

Another major point at which the new left and the direct action movement found themselves converging was the war in Vietnam. Whereas many liberals condemned the war and called for gradual withdrawal and disengagement, the new left demanded immediate withdrawal. Unwilling to join in the liberals' equal condemnation of both sides, the new left identified the United States as the only aggressor, seeking to perpetuate feudal landowning regimes at the expense of the land-hungry, revolutionary peasantry and waging a ruthless and genocidal war against a poor, nonwhite people. The direct action movement echoed these sentiments out of its established identification between American racism and overseas colonialism and out of a growing recognition that Negroes were being forced to carry a disproportionate burden in the war, both in terms of fighting men and casualties and in the form of cutbacks in federal programs to aid the poor. *Freedomways* commented:

> The Johnson Doctrine of policemanship over the struggling colonial peoples of the world is a racist colonialist policy. Consequently, it is a policy which is in fundamental conflict with and opposition to any genuine fulfillment of the long-overdue rights of Negro Americans.
>
> Especially are our youth made to feel the full weight of this policy. Too often they cannot find jobs, have no money to pay for a college education, and as a consequence face a choice of being drafted or volunteering for the Armed Forces as an escape from going hungry in the streets. For many, Vietnam is their graveyard.[26]

In July, 1965, the McComb branch of the Mississippi Freedom Democratic party issued an antiwar statement, which said:

> No one has the right to ask us to risk our lives and kill other Colored people in Santo Domingo and Vietnam, so that the White American can get richer. We will be looked upon as traitors by all the Colored people of the world if the Negro people continue to fight and die without a cause.[27]

The Student Nonviolent Coordinating Committee took the position that the government was deceptive in claiming to guarantee freedom in Vietnam and the Dominican Republic because "Our work, particularly in the South, has taught us that the United States Government has never guaranteed the freedom of oppressed citizens, and is not yet truly determined to end the rule of terror and oppression within its own borders." [28] Even the more moderate and generally pro-administration leader Martin Luther King issued sharp criticism of the war.

On yet another front, radicalizing forces were moving CORE toward a break with its old alliances. Continuing racist violence in the South and increasing need to appeal to the angry mood of the Northern ghetto were undermining the organization's commitment to nonviolence, as it has been discussed in this book. Most specifically and immediately the change was foreshadowed by the organization of the "Deacons for Self-Defense" in Bogalusa, Louisiana. The Negro community in this southern Louisiana town had been organized by CORE during the summers of 1963 and 1964. Civil rights activities had been plagued by constant and severe violence by Klan members and white mobs. In 1965 a group of Negro adults organized an armed self-defense organization to protect the Negro community from attack. The CORE-backed Bogalusa Voters League was closely connected with this defense unit, and CORE workers traveled and organized under the wing of its armed membership.[29] Bogalusa was merely the outstanding case. Wherever indigenous Southern Negro community organizations began to replace integrated CORE groups from the outside, self-defense was increasingly accepted. In the Northern ghettos, CORE organizers found that the doctrine of nonviolence was a positive liability, clashing, as it did, with the mood of the ghetto inhabitants.

The new left's condemnation of American society as unreformable and its decisive break with the liberal Democrats, the administration, organized labor, the established universities—in short, its break from the whole "liberal establishment"—played directly into the growing trend toward Negro nationalism in the direct action movement. To the new left, the liberal establishment was suspect because it was bureaucratic, materialistic, and tainted by its close association with big business and the military.[30] To the Negro activists trying to reach the ghetto masses, the establishment was suspect because it was white. The social criticism of the new left appealed to these activists because it gave additional substance to what they already felt and knew from their experiences with Southern FBI agents and Kennedy-appointed Southern federal judges and what the Negro masses knew from their years of total racial isolation in the ghetto: that the liberal establishment was out of touch with the reality of Southern tyranny and Northern ghetto misery.

Strained Alliance with the Liberal Establishment

In the civil rights movement, the new currents of radicalism expressed themselves most strongly in a desire to break with the Democratic party and other allies in the liberal establishment. The pros and cons of this break were argued with particular cogency by Bayard Rustin and Staughton Lynd. Rustin, one of the early CORE activists, former executive secretary to Martin Luther King, and one of the organizers of the march on Washington, urged that the civil rights movement now confront such problems as urban decay, automation, and poor schools. These issues, though connected with Jim Crow, required a larger framework for their solution. To change these conditions, the movement would have to make alliances with labor and liberal groups in order to garner the sheer numbers required to bring about effective governmental action:

> The future of the Negro struggle depends on whether the contradictions of this society can be resolved by a coalition of progressive forces which becomes the *effective* political majority in the United States. I speak of the coalition which staged the march on Washington, passed the civil rights act, and laid the basis for the Johnson landslide—Negroes, trade unionists, liberals, and religious groups.[31]

Rustin maintained that American democracy was still a viable path to basic, even revolutionary, reforms. He saw a beginning toward such reforms in civil rights legislation and the war on poverty. He accused those who turned their back on this course of adopting a "no win" philosophy and of substituting radical rhetoric for practical political action. Rustin's views were in substantial agreement with the position of Martin Luther King, still the most prominent spokesman of the direct action movement.

Staughton Lynd, one of the leading intellectual spokesmen of the new left, countered that the political majority of which Rustin spoke was already in power and had led the nation into the disastrous Vietnam war while fumbling ineffectually with problems of racism and poverty. Rustin's coalition, argued Lynd, would "assimilate Negro protest to the Establishment, just as labor protest was coopted at the end of the 1930s in each case leaving the poorest, least organized parts of the population out in the cold." [32] Such a coalition, he added, would mute criticism of foreign policy in return for minor gains in domestic policy. It would overlook the terrible price being paid by Negroes and the poor for the Vietnamese war. Further, it was an elitist position, because it assumed that major political decisions were to be made by agreements among leaders. The problems of the Negro, as of the whole society, could only be solved, Lynd argued, by a fundamental democratization of institutions, which would bring the nation back from its current situation in "a twilight zone between democratically delegated authority and something accurately called 'facism.'" [33]

Emergence of Black Power

At the 1966 CORE convention in Baltimore, all the radicalizing trends of the past several years converged and exploded, precipitating a clear break with CORE's nonviolent, integrationist past. Many of the long-time white members were conspicuously absent.* The convention was 60 to 70 percent Negro. It was presided over by Floyd McKissick, new executive director, who had taken over from James Farmer during the previous year. McKissick's rhetoric was strikingly more radical than Farmer's. Typical was his characterization of President Johnson as "the great white father [whose rhetoric] would make a rattlesnake cry." [34] Among the main speakers at the convention were Stokely Carmichael, head of SNCC and founder of the Black Panther party; Jesse Gray, radical leader of the New York rent strikes who during the Harlem riot had called for a hundred revolutionaries willing to die;[35] and Lonnie X, Black Muslim, who spoke on the problem of black identity. Martin Luther King, who had been scheduled as the main speaker, canceled after he heard of McKissick's intention to adopt black power as the theme of the convention.

Because black power is a slogan rather than an articulated doctrine, its adoption as the convention theme immediately gave rise to the most varied interpretations. Martin Luther King assailed the slogan as meaning "Black supremacy and black nationalism," [36] and Roy Wilkins, head of the NAACP, charged that "no matter how endlessly they try to explain it, the term 'black power' means anti-white power . . . It is a reverse Ku Klux Klan." [37]

In a position paper on black power, CORE leaders argued that the meaning of the slogan had been "twisted by knaves to make a trap for fools." The slogan, they said, had been misinterpreted to mean violence and racism because of the "malevolent Southern tradition that, even now seeks to divide Black Americans into 'good' and 'bad' niggers." [38] The paper maintained that black power was merely a slogan asserting the right of Negro Americans to do what all other groups in the society had done:

* Due to last-minute changes in the time and site, the delegates were overwhelmingly from the northeastern region. My data on the convention are insufficient to give information on precise splits in voting by race and region. Because most major votes were nearly unanimous, however, the overall composition of the convention is the best indication for the sources of support for the changes in policy it enacted.

It is singular that Black Americans, in the midst of their own revolution, have been made the subject of a new kind of ridicule and hatred emanating from our desire to do, at last, what the white community has always asked us to do—grab our bootstraps, consolidate our political power and act in the framework of this democracy to change our own lives.

This is Black Power—a concept as old as the first American immigrant who sought to share in the government of this land. As old as John Fitzgerald of Boston, Massachusetts, who built a base of political power that placed his grandson in the White House.[39]

The position paper made it clear that the black power concept did include the development of positive feelings about negritude:

It [black power] does not mean black separatism or the Black Muslims' approach. It means an honest recognition of the beauty of blackness and negritude, and an understanding of African history; an awareness of Negro culture and history within the American heritage, and a dedication to help create a new society rather than welcome Negroes into first-class citizenship in the old. It is further understood that Negro contributions will be as fundamentally important as white ones in the new creation.[40]

The same desire to appeal to the black masses, even at the cost of alienating white liberal allies, led the convention to change CORE's old position of dedication to nonviolence. In a near-unanimous vote, the convention adopted a resolution asserting that henceforth the doctrine of nonviolence would not be interpreted as abrogating the "natural and constitutional right of self-defense." As Floyd McKissick explained, "Negroes are not geared to nonviolence." [41] Referring to the unabating racist violence in the South and the continuing failure of local or federal authorities to bring it under control, he added, "The black man's cup is run over. I think the philosophy of nonviolence is a dying philosophy . . . No longer can you ask Negroes to adhere to nonviolence unless you call on whites to be nonviolent." [42]

Interpretations of the meaning of the new position were as varied and conflicting as the debate over black power. Former national director James Farmer said that he saw no change of policy in the resolution. CORE, he stated, had never taken a stand on the Negro's right to defend himself and his home from attack; it had only adopted nonviolence as a rule governing the conduct of demonstrations. This, Farmer asserted, had not been changed by the resolution.[43] In his book *Freedom When?* published a year earlier, Farmer had, indeed, defended the self-defense organization, the Deacons, as a move warranted by the conditions in Louisiana, where the concept of equal protection of the law had simply never existed.[44]

The current CORE leadership, however, interpreted the resolution as clearly applying to demonstrators under attack. In the words of the national chairman, Will Ussery, "All we did was let the police know that, if we are attacked, we won't just crouch down in our nonviolent position and sing 'We Shall Overcome' anymore." [45] National director McKissick even opened the possibility of retaliatory violence when he told the press, "Let the Ku Klux Klan come down the street and start bombing churches and homes, they are gonna get some bombing back." [46]

The change on nonviolence came under attack from the NAACP and various liberals, including some former CORE supporters. Lillian Smith, noted Southern author, resigned from her position on CORE's executive committee, charging in her resignation statement that "CORE has been infiltrated by adventurers, by nihilists, black nationalists and plain old fashioned haters, who have finally taken over." [47] Martin Luther King rejected the new policy but felt challenged to call for a stronger nonviolent alternative, something that "avoids violence, but becomes militant and extreme enough to disrupt the flow of a city." [48]

The convention also passed a strong resolution calling for an end to the Vietnamese war—the first statement in CORE's history taking a position on a nonracial issue. Again, the vote was nearly unanimous.

The full meaning of CORE's new position and direction is not yet clear. Does "black power" mean the virtual exclusion of whites from the organization? McKissick categorically denied such an intent,[49] yet the move toward ghetto organization leads naturally in that direction. The percentage of whites in elected and administrative positions had declined steadily since 1961. The National Action Council, the executive organ of CORE, contained only one white member by 1966 and only a few whites were still employed on the national staff.[50] A mood of hostility toward all whites pervaded some Northern chapters and tended to discourage white participation. Stokely Carmichael certainly echoed the mood of some Negro activists when he said that "we want to get the whites off our backs. We do not want them around. Sure, we are losing contributions and so-called support. Well, we do not want it from whites who are then going to try and tell us what to do." [51]

Would the new direction mean tacit support of rioting in urban ghettos? Again McKissick denied such an intention. Farmer had, in fact, frequently argued that political organization and direct action were the only hope of channeling off Negro frustration and preventing riots, though he recognized that such activity might sometimes come unavoidably close to setting off sparks in the tense, aggression-filled slums.[52] Yet there doubtless were others who felt, with Carmichael, that "I do not call them riots. I call them rebellions. It is not for me to endorse, condone or condemn them. It seems to me that the people of a community have to decide how to overcome their own oppression, and if rebellion is the way, then that is the way and it is all right with me." [53]

Would the new direction mean a complete break with the Democratic party and white liberal allies? Again, the position was unclear. There was general agreement that ghetto organizers and Southern voter registration workers should seek to build politically conscious, independent black voting blocs. Many organizers fully intended to turn these blocs against local Democratic city organizations, but it was too early for most to look beyond this stage to a nationwide or third-party strategy.[54]

One aspect of the new direction was clear. The politically active, often intellectual and radical Negro leaders of CORE had decided to cast their lot with the Negro masses—regardless of how far this union might lead them from the white allies of the movement. After the convention, CORE began mass distribution in the Northern ghettos of a poster that read: "Support Black Power; send $1 to CORE." The implications were clear. CORE was trying to shift its financial base from the white liberals to the ghetto masses. It had already shifted its rhetoric and it knew that this shift would inevitably cost it white support. A concerted gamble had been taken and a new phase in CORE's development had begun.

NOTES

1. "Militants Take Over Student Coordinating Group," *The New York Times,* May 17, 1966, p. 22.
2. John Benson, "Interview with Stokely Carmichael," *The Black Panther Party* (New York: Merit Publishers, 1966), p. 25. (Pamphlet circulated by the Young Socialist Alliance.)
3. *Ibid.,* pp. 25–26.
4. *Ibid.,* p. 28.
5. George Breitman, ed., *Malcolm X Speaks* (New York: Merit Publishers, 1965), p. 22.
6. *Ibid.,* p. 54.
7. *Ibid.,* p. 69.
8. *Ibid.,* pp. 211–212.
9. "CORE Maps Drive in Bogalusa," *The New York Times,* July 5, 1965, p. 1; and James Farmer, *Freedom When?* (New York: Random House, 1965), pp. 182–190.
10. Thomas Brooks, "The Negro Movement: Beyond Demonstrations," *Dissent,* 12 (Winter, 1965), 15.
11. Charles E. Silberman, *Crisis in Black and White* (New York: Random House, 1964), pp. 224–248. For an analysis of the connection between Negro unemployment and general problems of the American economy, see Gunnar Myrdal, *Challenge to Affluence* (New York: Pantheon, 1963).
12. From a Department of Labor study; quoted in Mike Parker, "Watts: An Analysis," *The* [Berkeley] *Campus Correlator,* 1 (Fall, 1965), 16.
13. Thomas T. Pettigrew, *A Profile of the Negro American* (Princeton, N.J.: Van Nostrand, 1964), p. 150.
14. Farmer, *op. cit.,* pp. 172 ff.
15. Interview with Will Ussery, national chairman, July, 1966.
16. "CORE Reverses Call for Vietnam Pullout," *The New York Times,* July 6, 1965, p. 1.
17. Farmer, *op. cit.,* p. 111.
18. *Ibid.,* pp. 96–97.
19. Marvin Rich, "Civil Rights Strategy After the March," *New Politics,* 11 (Fall, 1963), 48.
20. Tom Hayden, quoted in Paul Jacobs and Saul Landau, *The New Radicals* (New York: Vintage Books, 1966), p. 34.
21. *Ibid.,* p. 33.
22. Tom Hayden, Norm Truchter, and Alan Cheuse, "Ideology, Communism, and Coalition," in *Studies on the Left* (Spring, 1965); quoted in Jacobs and Landau, *op. cit.,* pp. 267–268.
23. *Ibid.,* p. 62.
24. "The White House Conference and the Great Society" (editorial), *Freedomways,* 6 (Spring, 1966), 101–102.

25. Lou Smith, CORE West Coast field secretary, in *The* [Berkeley] *Campus Correlator,* 1 (Fall, 1965), 10.
26. "White House Conference," *op. cit.*
27. Jacobs and Landau, *op. cit.,* p. 249.
28. *Ibid.,* p. 251, quoted from SNCC statement "The U.S. Government Has Deceived Us" (ca. 1966).
29. Farmer, *op. cit.;* interview with Nancy Gilmore, CORE volunteer worker in Louisiana, summer, 1965; Sara Shumer, "Bogalusa, Year of Violence and Change," *The Movement,* 2 (February, 1966), 2.
30. *The Movement,* Vol. 2, No. 2 (February, 1966). (Published by California SNCC.)
31. Jacobs and Landau, *op. cit.,* pp. 305–306; Bayard Rustin, "From Protest to Politics: The Future of the Civil Rights Movement," *Commentary* (February, 1965).
32. Staughton Lynd, "Coalition Politics or Nonviolent Revolution?" *Liberation* (June–July, 1965), quoted in Jacobs and Landau, *op. cit.,* p. 311.
33. *Ibid.,* p. 316.
34. "Negro Leaders Split Over Policy," *The New York Times,* July 7, 1966, p. 1.
35. Farmer, *op. cit.,* p. 99.
36. "Black Power Is Black Death" (editorial), *The New York Times,* July 7, 1966, p. 34.
37. "Humphrey Backs NAACP Fight on Black Racism," *The New York Times,* July 7, 1966, p. 1.
38. "Congress of Racial Equality: Statement of Position on Black Power" (mimeographed, Summer, 1966). (Circulated by CORE.)
39. *Ibid.,* pp. 1–2.
40. *Ibid.,* p. 4.
41. "Director of CORE Criticizes Nonviolence as a Dying Principle," *The Los Angeles Times,* July 3, 1966, Sec. A, pp. 1, 20.
42. *Ibid.*
43. "Farmer Sees No Shift in Nonviolent Policy," *The Los Angeles Times,* July 3, 1966, Sec. A, p. 20.
44. Farmer, *op. cit.,* pp. 98–99.
45. Interview with Will Ussery, July, 1966.
46. "Director of CORE Criticizes," *op. cit.*
47. "CORE Is Assailed by Lillian Smith," *The New York Times,* July 6, 1966, p. 16.
48. "Dr. King Asserts Rights Movement Is 'Close to Split,'" *The New York Times,* July 9, 1966, p. 1.
49. "CORE Chief Assails Humphrey for His Attack on Black Power," *The New York Times,* July 8, 1966, p. 16.
50. Letter from Marvin Rich, July 28, 1966.
51. "'Black Power' Advocate Seeks Chicago Backing," *The Los Angeles Times,* July 29, 1966, p. 6.

52. Farmer, *op. cit.,* p. 33.
53. " 'Black Power' Advocate," *op. cit.*
54. Interview with Louis Smith, West Coast field secretary for CORE, July, 1966.

CORE . . . Rules for Action

CORE and Nonviolence

CORE, the Congress of Racial Equality, is a national organization with affiliated local groups, committed to the goal of erasing the color line through methods of direct nonviolent action. All groups affiliated with national CORE agree to follow the nonviolent procedure in all action which they sponsor.

NONVIOLENCE has been shown to be a powerful social force. A threefold type of power characterizes nonviolence: (1) the power of active good will and nonretaliation; (2) the power of public opinion against an injustice; (3) the power of refusing to be a party to injustice, as illustrated by the boycott and the strike.

SINCERE INDIVIDUALS all over the world have used this tactic to overcome seemingly overwhelming odds. When used by a dedicated group trained to understanding and personal discipline, it can change the social order.

THE NONVIOLENT DIRECT ACTION APPROACH to problems of racial discrimination assumes that a lasting resolution of problems can best be obtained through a spirit of good will and understanding. This spirit must be combined with a determination to end discrimination through action programs directed to specific problems. The ultimate goal is an integrated society where each member is judged solely on the basis of his individual worth.

CORE urges that members should not knowingly participate in any situation involving segregation unless there is no other choice or unless they are participating in action toward elimination of discrimination.

Guarantees of the Individual to the Group

1. A CORE member will investigate the facts carefully before determining whether or not racial injustice exists in a given situation.

2. A CORE member will seek at all times to understand both the attitude of the person responsible for a policy of

racial discrimination, and the social situation which engendered the attitude. The CORE member will be flexible and creative, showing a willingness to participate in experiments which seem constructive, but being careful not to compromise CORE principles.

3. A CORE member will make a sincere effort to avoid malice and hatred toward any group or individual.

4. A CORE member will never use malicious slogans or labels to discredit any opponent.

5. A CORE member will be willing to admit mistakes.

6. He will meet the anger of any individual or group in the spirit of good will and creative reconciliation: he will submit to assault and will not retaliate in kind either by act or word.

7. A member will never engage in any action in the name of the group except when authorized by the group or one of its action units.

8. When in an action project a CORE member will obey the orders issued by the authorized leader or spokesman of the project, whether these orders please him or not. If he does not approve of such orders, he shall later refer the criticism back to the group or to the committee which was the source of the project plan.

9. No member, after once accepting the discipline of the group for a particular action project, shall have the right of withdrawing. However, should a participant feel that under further pressure he will no longer be able to adhere to the *Rules for Action,* he shall then withdraw from the project and leave the scene immediately after notifying the project leader.

10. Only a person who is a recognized member of the group or a participant accepted by the group leader in a particular project shall be permitted to take part in that group action.

11. Each member has the right to dissent from any group decision and, if dissenting, need not participate in the specific action planned.

12. Each member shall understand that all decisions on general policy shall be arrived at only through democratic group discussion.

13. A CORE member shall receive the uncompromising support of his CORE group as he faces any difficulties resulting from his authorized CORE activities.

APPENDIX **II**

Convention Questionnaires

Questionnaire Used at Cincinnati Convention, Winter, 1961

Race?   Sex?   Age?
Religious affiliation?
How many times a month do you attend church?
Father's religious affiliation?
Mother's religious affiliation?
Years of education completed?
Your occupation at present?
   (if unemployed, give your last regular occupation)
Father's occupation?
   (or occupation of person who was your guardian when you
   were a minor)
CORE chapter of which you are presently a member?
Do you hold any office in the local chapter or national organi-
   zation? Please list offices:
When did you first join CORE?
Before you joined CORE, were you a member of any other
   Integration Organizations?
Which ones?
To what other organizations do you presently belong? List all
   organizations: political, professional, recreational, etc. When
   listing local groups whose names may not be well known,
   please indicate purpose or type of group it is:
Have you been arrested in connection with integration ac-
   tivities?

Questionnaire Used at Miami Convention, Summer, 1962

Race?   Sex?   Age?   Marital Status?
Place of birth?
Religious affiliation?
   (put denomination: Methodist, etc.)
Father's religious affiliation?   Mother's?

How many times a month do you attend church?

Years of education completed?

Your present occupation?
   (if unemployed, give your last regular occupation)

Father's occupation?
   (or occupation of person who was your guardian when you were a minor)

CORE chapter of which you are presently a member?

Do you hold any office in the local chapter or national organization? Please list offices.

When did you first join CORE?
   (give year and month)

Before you joined CORE, were you a member of any other Integration Organizations?

Which ones?

To what other organizations do you presently belong? List all organizations: political, professional, recreational, etc. When listing local groups whose names may not be well known, please indicate purpose or type of group it is.

Have you been arrested in connection with integration activities?

Interview Data Sheet

Type Interview?
Race?   Sex?   Age?   Marital status?   Children?
Residential arrangement?
  (type, with whom, ownership)
Place of birth?   Size of town?
Religion?
Church attendance per month?
Father's religion?
Mother's religion?
Years of school completed?
College major?
Occupation?
  (present or last regular)
What do you hope to be doing occupationally in ten years?
How much money do you expect to be making at this?
Father's (or guardian's) occupation?
Offices presently held in local or national CORE?
Past CORE offices?
Residence history?
Political party affiliation?
Father's (or guardian's) income?
Father's (or guardian's) education?
Size of firm in which Father works?   Union member?
Mother's occupation?

Member Interview

Getting into CORE

When did you first get into CORE? [get month and year if possible—get some idea of how long person was a probationary member—when he became an active member.]

How did you first get interested in CORE? [find out what kinds of personal contacts got respondent in—how much he had heard through newspapers, etc.]

Did you belong to any other Civil Rights groups previously?

WHITES: How did you first get interested in the integration issue? [How do your parents feel about it? etc.]

NEGROES: Why do you think that you, in particular, have become so active in an organization like this? [Probe: How old were you when the Supreme Court decision on school desegregation was handed down? Do you remember what the expectations of people around you—and your own—were at that time?]

Involvement in CORE

How many hours a week do you spend in CORE activities [including meetings, action projects, errands, etc.]?

How does this compare with other organizations you spend time in [include church and social organizations here]?

How important to you is CORE compared to other organizations you are in?

Do you hold offices in the group? Are you on committees? Have you attended national conventions, national workshops, etc.?

Do you see CORE people socially, outside of CORE? How many of them are close friends?

Were these people friends before, or did you meet them in CORE?

How long will you continue to be active in CORE?

[Do you expect to stay in the South?]

Does being a CORE member affect the way you feel and act when you are just out on your own? [Probe for codes of behavior like breaking seating patterns on buses, reacting differently to difficult incidents with whites, etc.]

Goals and Time Perspective

[Give graph and time-check list—note all comments made while this is being filled out.]

Prior to letting respondent fill out graph, ask and mark on graph:

1. When do you think Negroes will reach full citizenship (in the whole country)?

2. Considering that we started from slavery about 100 years ago, do you think we have come halfway to full citizenship? How far?

3. Has it been a steady progress over the last 100 years or were there ups and downs? Or was there a sudden upswing? When did the upswing take place?

4. Which movements prior to 1960 do you think were important in fighting for civil rights? (Now let them fill out graph, being careful that they actually follow the main lines of opinions expressed above.)

[Now give time-check list.]

[Probe: Why did you choose these items as most important?]

What do you think of CORE's emphasis on public accommodations? If you didn't choose it as important, why didn't you?

*　　　*　　　*

If the integration movement is successful, what kind of society do you think will emerge here in the South? [Or, how do you think your own life will be changed?]

[Watch for: ideological vs. "bread and butter" orientation; personally oriented vs. impersonal view.]

[After allowing spontaneous expression, probe for whether the person thinks other problems will change also: the general quality of politics in the South; wage levels, unionization; welfare standards; cultural standards; etc.]

[Watch here whether other present evils are laid at door of segregation? Shut out of view? etc.]

Important Experiences

Which of your CORE activities or experiences have you found most satisfying?

[Allow a description of the event—probe for sources of satisfaction, effect on respondent's outlook, etc.]

Have you had any experiences with insults, violence, or jail?

[Probe: How did you react to being in jail—how was it? Did it deepen your involvement in CORE? How did your family take it? Friends, teachers, or other important persons?]

Ideology of Nonviolent Direct Action

How have you become familiar with nonviolence?

[Check for reading (specific references); workshops, conventions, etc.; contacts with local members, national officers, etc.]

Do you consider nonviolence a tactic or a personal ethic?

Have you thought about being a conscientious objector in war?

Have you changed your thinking about nonviolence since being in CORE?

Have you had experiences where you were afraid you might not stay nonviolent?

In what ways do you think nonviolence is an effective method? Whom does it influence?

[Further probes: If the next twenty years don't bring real results, do you think people will begin to turn to violent means? What do you think of the claim of the black nationalists that nonviolence is just another expression of the Negro's passive role?

Do you prefer mass-participation with loose discipline, or would you rather see a small, highly disciplined group doing the direct action?]

Negro-White Relations in CORE

NEGRO: Is there a difference in what motivates whites and Negroes to become active in CORE?

Is there more of a turnover on white members? Why?

Are the white members as willing to picket, go to jail, etc.?

Do you ever feel uncomfortable about the way the whites do things? About their attitudes?

Why, in your opinion, are the white people in CORE different from most Southern whites?

What would you say is the difference between "white liberals" and white CORE members?

WHITE: Is there a difference in what motivates whites and Negroes to become active in CORE? Is there a difference in the types of people that join from each racial group?

Is it possible for whites to be really "in" this struggle, or do you feel whites are relegated to the position of "allies"?

Is there a tendency to prefer Negroes for leadership positions? Do you feel bothered by this?

Do you feel the Negroes tend to have a narrower political outlook—sort of a sole emphasis on the race problem?

Are you ever worried that there are some sensitivities of the Negro members that you don't understand and might injure?

Do you ever wish you were a Negro?

When you are just out by yourself and something happens that makes you feel uncomfortable about being white—do you get this feeling more since you have been in CORE?

Do you feel uncomfortable about using segregated facilities?

Leadership

What qualities are most important in a good CORE chairman? Which of the chairmen you have had was best? Why? What do you think of James Farmer as a national leader?

CORE's Relation to the Community

Are there any other Civil Rights groups here which you feel are doing an effective job? How about nationally?

What do you think people outside CORE think of it: The older Negro leadership? Liberal whites? Segregationists? The average Negro?

Leader Interview

Founding of Chapter and Freedom Ride Period

When was the chapter founded?

What kinds of people were in on the founding? Did National staff persons come in?

Was it founded in response to a particular situation?

[During the Freedom Ride period:] Did the membership increase? Was there a change in the type of membership you got? What did the chapter do on the Freedom Ride project?

Membership and Turnover

[If possible, take the membership list and have chairman designate for each member: Race, age, occupation, and offices held in the group.

Find out which members have come in during the last six months. How much has membership increased (or decreased) in last six months? (Figure the rate of turnover: number of new members minus number of increase.)]

What kinds of people do you lose and why?

Through what kinds of contacts or activities do you get new members? Do you do any sort of organized membership recruiting? Who is in charge of this?

How many local associate members do you have? What do you call on them for?

What is the procedure for becoming an active member? [Has anyone ever been turned down?]

Major Direct Action Projects

What have been your main direct action projects during the past year?

FOR EACH: In response to what situation were they initiated? What did you have to do to prepare for the direct action phase of the project? [In negotiations, are people becoming more willing to recognize CORE as a bargaining agent?]

Have any projects been carried out in conjunction with other organizations? Has this held up direct action?

Has the group been asked to hold off direct action because of other things going on in the civil rights area? How has this been handled?

Have you had any discipline problems in your direct action projects? How handled? How many arrests have you had in connection with the projects?

What has been the tangible outcome of each project?

Broader Participation Activities (Fund-Raising Events, Rallies, Etc.)

How do you promote these events? What kind of advertising and community and group contacts do you use?

From what segment of the community do you draw support?

What is CORE's image in various parts of the Negro and white communities, in your opinion?

Mass Participation Activities (Boycotts, Mass Marches, Very Large Direct Action, Etc.)

Is there a letdown in the group when mass support ebbs away? How is this handled?

Do members keep a distinction in their minds between the CORE group and the temporary activists?

Is there a sense of elite-group leadership?

Do you as a chairman prefer actions where you use only your members or actions using mass participation?

Members

What kinds of activities are best for the members' morale?

What kind of things do you have the most trouble getting people who are qualified for, out of your membership?

Facing arrest or violence? Routine things—secretarial, mailing lists, etc.? Things requiring education—negotiating, writing, speaking? Taking leadership or responsibility?

Are some people in the chapter more conservative than others on most issues? Are there any other kinds of systematic splits? [What kinds of people are on which side?]

Chapter Structure and Leadership in the Chapter

What kinds of officers and committees are really operating?

How much time per week do you spend at meetings and in activities and chores for CORE?

Outside of official business, how much time do you spend with CORE members informally? Were these people personal friends before you joined CORE?

Do these people make up the active group within CORE? How stable is this group? What determines who gets into this group?

Suppose you had a direct action project scheduled and some important last-minute decision came up [for example, whether to postpone action because of possible violence]. Whom would you consult? Does the constitution require you to consult anyone?

How are the chapter's finances?

Do you ever put money out for things without expecting to get it back? How do you handle getting treasury funds for expenses? What kind of records does the Chapter keep? What kinds of records are kept of other activities—minutes of meetings, records of negotiations, legal proceedings, correspondence, contact lists, etc.?

Where are the records kept [see them if possible]?

From your own experience, what would you say are the most important qualities a person needs to be a good chairman?

Contacts with the National Organization

How frequent are your telephone and mail contacts with New York?

Have you ever stopped an undertaking because of the attitude of the national office?

How many members do you send to action institutes, conventions, etc.?

Do you have any kicks about how the national office operates —about their policies and projects?

Is there a field secretary in the area? How closely do you work with him? Is there any conflict of authority there? How do you perceive the division of labor between yourself and the field secretary?

List for other interviews.

Sample CORE Chapters'
Regional Representation

Northern Chapters: Interview Data

St. Louis	Berkeley
Seattle	Los Angeles
Oakland	San Jose

Northern Chapters: Questionnaire Data

Detroit	Ann Arbor
Long Island	Brooklyn
Chicago	St. Louis
Los Angeles	Columbus
Washington, D.C.	Newark
Berkeley	Cincinnati
New Haven	Syracuse
Alton, Ill.	Manhattan
Staten Island	Boston
Kansas City	

Southern Chapters: Interview Data

Miami
New Orleans
Baton Rouge
Jackson
Louisville

Southern Chapters: Questionnaire Data

East St. Louis	Northern Virginia
Baton Rouge	Covington
New Orleans	Houston
Suffolk, S.C.	Northern Kentucky
Miami	Jackson

Louisville
Columbia, S.C.
Greensboro
High Point, N.C.

Shreveport
Baltimore
Lexington

Index

Kahn, Tom, 50n, 51–52
Karon, Bertram, 132
Killian, Lewis, 64, 156–157
King, Martin Luther, 8, 11, 31, 33, 36–38, 47, 106, 117n, 138, 175, 184–187, 189
Kraft, Joseph, 60

Left-wing ideology and CORE, 29, 46, 50–53, 55, 138–139, 167–168, 177
Lenski, Gerhard, 128–129
Lewis, John, 175
Lomax, Louis, 7
Lynd, Staughton, 185–186

Malcolm X, 50, 176–177
March on Washington (1963), 5, 11
McCain, Jim, 9
McKissick, Floyd, 187, 189–190
Mississippi Freedom Democratic party, 12–13, 175, 184
"Moderate type," 120–124; access to radical ideas of, 138–139; case study of, 143–146; race and, 126, 166; region of, 126, 131–137, 139; religion of, 138; socioeconomic status of, 129–130, 139, 132–134
Myrdal, Gunnar, 29–30, 191n

National Association for the Advancement of Colored People (NAACP), 4–6, 10, 12, 52, 138, 187, 189; and Robert Williams, 46, 54, 60, 62. *See also* CORE
Negro dominance of CORE, 152–155, 164, 166, 189–190
Negro identity, 7, 47–49, 83, 108–118, 140, 142, 178, 180, 188
Negro unemployment, 5, 52, 173, 178, 180, 183–184
Negro protest, history of, 3–7
Negroes, migration of, 6–7
New left, influence of, 16, 181–186
New York World's Fair project, 13–14
Nonviolence, 26, 37, 51, 118–120; and American culture, 36–38, 109, 118, 120, 163, 169, 171; as CORE ideology, 32–33, 36, 37–41, 169–174, 195–196; and CORE whites,

162–163; degree of commitment to, 105–108, 169–174; as legitimation, 36–38, 43–44, 58–59, 169–171; and moderate-radical typology, 118, 120, 143, 144; and Negro passivity, 47, 109, 111–118, 132, 144; and Negro psychology, 37–39, 169, 172; and regional difference, 111–115; rejection of, 15, 17, 27–28, 48, 57, 108, 113–118, 143, 164–165, 169–171, 174, 177, 184–189; and socioeconomic status, 80, 109–111, 114; and white liberals, 57, 59
Nonviolent discipline, 110–113, 116–117, 195–196
"Nonviolent type," 120–124; access to radical ideas, 138–139; race of, 126, 166–168; region of, 126, 131–137, 139; religion of, 138; socioeconomic status of, 129–130, 132, 134, 139

Pacifist influence in CORE, 9, 20, 32–35, 42, 66, 107–108, 118–120, 139, 146, 164, 169
Police brutality, 11, 86, 116, 158, 161, 166, 178
Political style and racial difference, 127, 166–168
Primary group ties in CORE, 76–77, 79, 90–92, 150, 152, 156–158

Quakers, 9, 26, 33, 34–35

Racism, 51, 55, 59–60, 169, 171, 176–177, 182, 184
"Radical type," 120–124; access to radical ideas, 138–139, 140–141; case study of, 139–143; race of, 126, 166, 168; region of, 126, 131–137, 139; religion of, 138; socioeconomic status of, 129–130, 132–134, 139
Relative deprivation, 128, 132
Rich, Marvin, 39n
Rustin, Bayard, 14, 181, 185–186

Searles, Ruth, 89n
Segregation: establishment of, 3–4; unconstitutionality of, 6, 29, 31